BECOMING A
RELATIONAL
FIRST RESPONDER

Using Six
Bond Building Expressions

Vinny Gerace

Confia Publishers is the publishing ministry for the Centers of Church Based Training, an international ministry focused on encouraging the local church to bring all to maturity and many to leadership through an intentional pathway. Confia Publishers is committed to partnering with local churches in providing biblically based, culturally relevant and highly practical resources to help individuals and groups in local churches to mature in Christ.

For more information please go to:

ccbt.org and confiapublishers.org or call toll-free 888-422-2896.

ISBN: 978-1-943373-05-5

© Copyright Vinny Gerace All rights reserved.

2022 Confia Publishers, a ministry of Centers of Church Based Training.

Printed in the United States of America

Centers of Church Based Training
2801 Orchid Dr., McKinney, Texas 75070

toll-free: 888-422-2896
email: customersupport@ccbt.org

CONTENT

Dedication /1

Acknowledgements /3

Introduction: The Big Idea /5

Chapter ONE – Four Core Principles /7

Chapter TWO – The House Model /17

Chapter THREE – Becoming a Good "First Responder" /39

Chapter FOUR – Four Practice Accidents /71

Chapter FIVE – "Easter Eggs" for Relational Growth, /77
            a Baker's Dozen

Chapter SIX – Epilogue: My Journey as a First Responder /89

Dedication

There comes a time when you realize there is less time ahead of you than there is behind you, and people you love will outlast you and will need the wisdom you have. When this idea took hold in me, I realized that the hard-won principles in this book would fade with me and not benefit them if I didn't write them down. Those principles would need to be relearned through all the same struggles, and that does not need to happen. Nor would I condemn anyone to live my life to relearn them.

So, this book is dedicated to Andrew (my son) and to all my grandchildren—especially Alexis, who begged me to write this. I also dedicate this book to my wife Teresa without whom I would struggle in all things. You put up with my abstractness and a thousand other things as I wrote this book. You are an awesome and fearless person with the highest integrity. You are all my inspiration.

Acknowledgements

I want to acknowledge Dr. Taibi Kahler (for the Process Communication Model and his understanding of personality and motivation) and to Drs. Joe and Judy Pauley, who taught me those concepts so well. The Six "Expressions" described in this book are a "less technical" reflection of his work in categorizing communication and personality types. I also recognize no book is ever produced with the help of a host of other people. So, I also acknowledge the help of my illustrators, editors, and all those who made my writing intelligible, and to the publishers, who labored through the book creation process with me,
thank you all.

Introduction: The Big Idea

Have you ever said something in anger to someone that seemed completely true at that moment but later seemed like an exaggeration? I have, and after talking with many people, I have found that's a pretty common experience. Unfortunately, I have also discovered that many of us carry forward those exaggerated emotions into future encounters with that same person. We find difficulty using our knowledge about the exaggerated emotions and may view that relationship negatively during future encounters.

I became intrigued by *why* this happens and became engrossed in a fifteen-year-long examination about *how it happens* and *how to stop it*. What I found is the big idea of this book. This book offers a set of ideas, principles, and best practices that have been distilled into a focused method that helps people remember you in a positive light, even when they don't get what they want from you.

All people relate to you in order to satisfy needs and reasons that are personal to themselves. So, when your way of expressing yourself aligns with those needs at three very specific moments in their interaction with you, they have a high likelihood to remember the engagement (and you) in a positive way. This holds true even if they did not receive what was expected or desired.

I was always taught to meet people's expectations in order to create a positive bond with them. I found this particularly difficult when (for whatever reason) I chose to disappoint their expectations or failed to meet their expectations. While I was exhausting myself trying to meet the expectations of those around me, I watched others—who failed to meet expectations at least as much (if not more) than I did—move into greater and greater levels of trust and bondedness.

My journey has helped me develop the House Model with its three downward-leading layers of relational distress and three upward-leading layers of relational unity. During my research to clarify how this continuum worked, I ran into the Process Communication Model (PCM), which described in great detail how and why those three layers of decent into distress happen for each personality type. Dr. Taibi Kahler created PCM, and his work allowed me to take the House Model and refine it into the process presented in this book.

The big idea in this book revolves around the discovery of *how* you store (remember) relational-status information and set the emotional boundaries and attitudes around relationships. I will also explain how to weight that process in your favor. But first we need to look at the House Model and the principles that support it.

Chapter ONE – Four Core Principles

Principle 1: Relationships are about personal satisfaction; it's all about you.

People are driven relationally by reasons specific to themselves. Most of your relationships are born out of life circumstances that you did not orchestrate. Finding ourselves in relationships, we each feel a desire to receive some benefit for ourselves out of those relationships. Each person creates this desire out of their need for—something. Understanding this "something" is an inseparable and critically important foundation in any relationship.

This "something" does not emerge from a vacuum but rather is drawn from a driving need within the psyche of the individual. This means that people are motivated relationally by factors within themselves. In fact, most people's relationships revolve around attempts to satisfy or create these benefits: whatever motivates and satisfies you relationally. Understanding these needs and motivations helps us deal with relational choices, loyalties, relational failure, relational losses, relational commitments, and a host of other relational dynamics.

Most people operate on autopilot in that they are unaware in the moment of the things that they need or want from others. Yet this tacit need inspires their engagement (or disengagement) and determines the level of their satisfaction (or dissatisfaction). Whether we have awareness of these needs or not, they influence our actions both overtly and subtly.

The good news is (as complex as people are) there isn't an infinite set of variables that defines human motivational needs and attachment avenues. When relationships feed into these motivational needs, we are drawn to others and satisfied by our relationship with them. Conversely, when relationships fail to meet these desires, we experience disappointment, rejection, and negative relational feedback that causes us to push away from those relationships.

Most importantly, this reminds us that relationships work because of *who others perceive us to be* **to them**. To say this another way, how the other person perceived you in *their* mental-emotional drama is more important relationally than who you intended to be to them.

Principle 2: Relationships are about limits and boundaries; it's never about you.

According to principle 1, we are relationally "all about ourselves," but according to principle 2, we don't get to be all about ourselves when we relate to another person. So, what can we do about that conflict? We remember that relationships are like a race. Races have starting blocks, lanes, and finish lines. And yes, a race has winners and losers.

The starting blocks are the same for everyone because everyone desires the same three things:
- We want to do what we want to do.
- We want to feel what we want to feel.
- We want to think what we want to think.
    - And we want to do so without resistance from others.
    - In fact, we really want their agreement and applause.

These desires set up two very big problems:
1. **Bad Things:** Many of the things we think, feel, and do are destructive to ourselves, our communities, and those around us! Even knowing that the desired action

will destroy something good or better, we might still think it, feel it, or do it!
2. **Limited Resources:** There are three basic categories of resources: time, talents, and things. Many of the things we think, feel, and do use a disproportionate amount of resources or demand the use of other people's resources! While it feels right to us for the resources to be used in this way, others who must surrender their resources (or use that same resource) experience a resource deficit that affects the satisfaction of their desires.

These problems create a situation where others will not accept our thoughts, feelings, or actions. So, people resist, correct, or even retaliate against these desires. They also set up rules and guidelines for each group and community, including punishments for crossing the line with our thoughts, feelings, and actions.

So, where does this leave us concerning our relational desires? Relating to others means encountering the resistance, correction, rejection, and conflict that we do not want. Relating to others means *limits*: tempering our desires with negotiation and self-control.

In relationships that last long-term, an acceptable level of give-and-take must be developed. Sometimes the needs of person A are deeply satisfied, and the needs of person B are less satisfied, and vice versa.

Most relationship books give their advice in these limited areas: satisfaction, fairness, negotiation, communication, and character. That is where the things that guide everyone relationally are described. In these books, principles like grace, forgiveness, grief, love, transparency, authenticity, and a host of others are exhaustively explained and illustrated.

However, such books and the methods they offer are often based on *assumptions* concerning people, and thus they fail for some. Such books work best with those who are willing, self-aware, and self-controlled. But they fail miserably with those who are unethical, brutal, or immature. For such people, failure to thrive relationally is certain.

This principle of communal limits says that while each individual is motivated to pursue their own satisfaction, we will not all reach satisfaction without curtailing the scope of choices for all members of the community through mutually agreed to limits. This is called interdependence. To accomplish interdependence, our relational choices should be focused on three things:

- Meeting the needs of others;
- Defending and negotiating limits (boundaries) concerning our resources; and
- Expressing and surrendering our desires to others for mutual satisfaction.

These three kinds of choices allow us to live in community with others and to meet our relational desires in protected relationships. While not every relationship or every relational exchange will bring satisfaction, we trust that through the reciprocal ebb and flow of relational dynamics within the whole community, everyone's core relational needs will eventually be satisfied through the relationships of all the community's members as they live and make choices within communal boundaries.

This is more than an ideal or hope; it also represents a pragmatic limit of relational-emotional health that leads to hard personal choices. Not all communities can satisfy all needs. When people ignore these relational rules and exceed the limits of a community's ability to support their needs, they find themselves ostracized, expelled, and even imprisoned. People will move from community to community trying to find a fit for themselves, and most do find their community. But some do not, or they do so with great suffering and difficulty.

So where do these limits leave us? They leave us understanding the scope of our choices. Our choices must fit within the limits and boundaries of the community, so others are free to pursue their needs, meet our needs, and vice versa. These limits also preserve our right to choose for ourselves what we will tolerate concerning our satisfaction, both personally and communally. As a human adult (who is not in a society that accepts slavery), you are not compelled to relate to any other adult. You may *feel* obligations, but those are usually beliefs and commitments that you have made that you resist breaking, not true compulsive obligations. I explained the communal limits and freedom of choice to pursue personal desires to my son when he was in 5th grade. I said:

> You want to do something, and I am telling you it is not acceptable, but you still want it, so you are willing to argue with me. You say it is your life and your choice, and you are right, *but* you live in a world of layers and limits.
>
> So, if you do not listen to your mother and I, there is another group of people: teachers, counselors, pastors, and others that will try to dissuade you. If you persist, there is another layer of people that will try to dissuade you by using harsher means: police officers, lawyers, mediators, and such. And finally, if you don't listen to any of us, your choices will be completely removed by the final level of human corrective authority in this community: juries, judges, and jailers.
>
> I assure you that it is better for you to adhere to my boundaries rather than those placed on you by the other layers because none of them have as much concern for you or your happiness as I do.

In the end, this principle says that if you live openly enough with enough people that most people will find their needs met to a satisfactory level. But *all* people (including ourselves) have limits to what they can accept personally and relationally. We can extrapolate from that acceptance to the social, organizational, and societal limits that bind us or break us.

The sense of connection we seek in community with others has rules and thresholds of acceptance. We perceive them as cold impersonal boundaries, but they are (in fact) rules set by the very human issues of limits and tolerance. Within societal structures there are sanctioned or sacred spaces developed to help protect the largest-mean-population's most common opportunities to build relational intimacy and connection. Knowing that some of these bonds take considerable time and effort to create, societies protect the growth of intimacy processes by setting apart these relationships and creating boundaries and repercussions for those who break them. Marriage is meant to safeguard; family is meant to safeguard; even friendship is meant to safeguard! They keep safe the opportunity to build and enjoy precious connections. When these societally sanctioned relationships are broken or abused, connections are strained, pained, and lost—sometimes for generations.

No *one* human person can satisfy your every need, and to be alone is not good for you. You were not built for it. You need people, and people need you. But relating with others is hard and fraught with conflict. But we should always remember: **more is gained through the work and pain of building unity with others than is lost in the process of building it.**

Principle 3: Relationships are made in moments *and* memories; it's all in your head.

People have amazing capacities and abilities, but they also have limits. One such limit is around our memory, so our brain simplifies experience in order to cohesively process life. People even simplify their memories about personal pain, joy, satisfaction, and self-reflection. They don't remember everything about an event or their experience of the event. I'm not talking about forgetting. I'm describing our ability to abbreviate the fullness of a memory into just a few words (if not a single word) or impressions. In fact, we don't remember everything about most things. In place of total recall, we remember categories, abstractions, and principles, so that we are not burdened by full, conscious memory.

Our relationships are subject to this truth about our limits. We can take a relationship that lasted years and condense it into a single feeling like fear, abandonment, love, camaraderie, or attraction. An entire relational history (or even an event within that relational history) can be abbreviated in understanding to a bond that is understood as a single word or idea.

We operate in a world of abbreviation! However, the experiences that underlie these bonds are very specific. When pulled apart and examined, we find there are specific moments that help us interpret the relational context. These moments form the abstraction (or our conception of the bond) that we think, feel, and act upon with the person. Our bonds, strengthened over time, build either more trust, forbearance, and transparency or more distrust, hurt, and dissatisfaction. To gain greater numbers in the kinds of relationships we desire, we must understand the relational continuum and the relational levels within it. This will also help us find greater relational satisfaction.

Principle 4: Relationships function within assumptions; it's all in your actions.

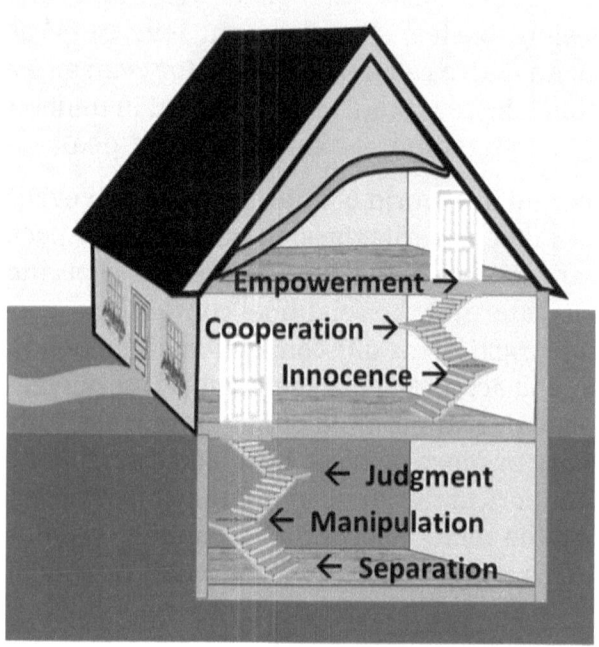

Figure 1: The House Model

Shopping malls are being replaced, but when I was a boy, I remember going to the mall, and the first thing I always wanted to do was go to the map and find the red dot. Next to that dot were the words "You are here." By looking at the map and the red dot, I could navigate my way to whatever store I wanted. Many years later, I recognized the pattern and progressive levels for relational unity and was able to lay out a map for relational connection. When I refined and clarified this continuum, I pictured a house with six steps (*see* Figure 1). Each step represents your relational status and its attendant and the disposition of your mind (attitude) toward the other person.

When you understand the House Model, it works as a map to help you navigate your way to where you want to go. All you need now is the red dot that says, "You are here." So, when you read through the description for each step, think about a specific person and ask yourself the question: where am I with this person? Every relationship you have is on one of these emotional steps. Everyone is on the map somewhere. This is *your* map; others don't have to place their relationship with you on the same step that you are experiencing with them. Everyone has their own map and their own red dot.

Remember, all relationships have an emotional position on one of the six steps. These steps govern your emotional expectations, interpretations, and perceptions. Each step contains different expectations. When we have a relationship on the Separation Step (at the bottom), we don't expect the same things that we would expect when a relationship stands on the Empowerment Step (at the top).

However, each time we encounter a new event within the relationship, our relational perception will either be reinforced (because it fits the step) or be challenged to move either *down* or *up* to the next step.

Movement either up or down always involves a purposeful (conscious) consideration about oneself and the other person, and movement happens when we are confronted by something *outside* of our step-defined-expectations. Movement on the steps is emotional **work** that *you* are doing, which often creates emotional hardship. While no one likes emotional hardship, people often choose to be passive and resist doing the work of changing their relational perceptions. This is how people get stuck **enduring** relational hardship rather than **changing** their emotional position for the better.

Moving down the steps involves greater internal pain and anguish, and moving up the steps requires more emotional work concerning self-awareness and self-acceptance. Due to our emotional inertia, we often find ourselves enduring terrible relational realities rather than confronting those realities.

Chapter TWO – The House Model

Downstairs – How We Get Down There and How to Get Out

We will start with the basement because we are very familiar with it. Seventy percent of the people polled claimed to be on the lower steps concerning seventy percent of the people they know, seventy percent of the time! This is a depressing statistic. This means people are struggling to find significant, positive, encouraging, and enjoyable relationships. The following three steps describe an ever-increasing decent into emotional isolation. We begin in Figure 1 at The Floor, which represents a midpoint on this relational continuum.

Step One (Going Down) Is Labeled the **Judgment** Step

When you stand on the Judgment Step, your mindset toward the other person is open but wary. Your expectation is that you don't know what will happen, but you don't expect it to be good, beneficial, or for you. You might desire the relationship to be positive, but you don't really expect it to be. This is a pessimistic mindset or a mindset with negative expectation. In this mental position, we interpret the actions and words of the other person through the lens of their-best-interest not our-mutual-best-interest. You don't believe they have considered you as anything more than a resource on the path to *their* satisfaction.

Psychologically speaking, you see them and what they are presenting to you as greater than you and your abilities. From a Transactional Analysis viewpoint, you have chosen to abdicate your adult state of mind and have positioned yourself for emotional combat.

To move _up_ a step, you must accomplish three mental and emotional objectives:

1. You must recognize that you are judging them (or their intent), and you must forgive yourself (and possibly ask for forgiveness from the other person) for your internal posture toward them.
2. You must acknowledge, confront, and verbalize _why_ and _how_ this failure to accept them (as a non-combatant) has happened within you.
3. You must resolve to disengage from Judgment, after having taken full control and responsibility for yourself and your circumstances. You must verbalize this positive mental and emotional resolution (at least to yourself and probably to them) by clarifying your relational intent toward them and the presenting circumstances.

Reminder: It is not enough to do these things mentally. You must do them _emotionally_! This is heart-level work to change your emotional disposition toward yourself and the circumstances presented to you by the other person.

If you don't do the work to move _up_ a step, then you will most likely act on your negative mindset. The moment you verbally, emotionally, or physically act with the other person _from this mindset,_ you will descend to the next lower step.

Step Two (Going Down) Is Labeled the **Manipulation** Step

When in Manipulation your mindset toward the other person is defensive and guarded. Your experience is that you have been attacked and your expectation is that _if_ you are going to get anything good out of this situation, you're going to have to fight for it. You may even think: "It didn't have to be this difficult." But you will see that as the other person's fault. This is a combative mindset, or a mindset that expects negative struggle to get what you deserve or to preserve your personal autonomy.

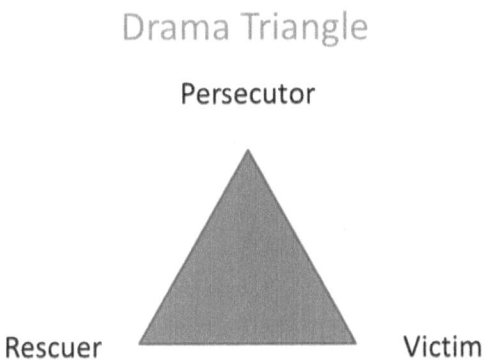

Figure 2: The Karpman Drama Triangle

In this mental and emotional position, we interpret the actions and words of the other people involved through the Karpman Drama Triangle. Dr. Steven Karpman's work on defining the positions in the drama triangle is seminal. Rather than taking responsibility for our mental state as a choice we made, we see our negativity as something "forced on us" by the other person. This is called taking the Victim role.

In this drama we are inventing, we cast the primary role of Persecutor on the person that has confronted us with the undesired expectation or perception. If the reality of personal choice and responsibility starts to invade our drama, third parties are engaged to collude with us (the Victim) to strengthen our position. This provides us with added security in our fantasy by confirming that the Persecutor is truly persecuting us and that we are truly a Victim. In so doing the third parties become Rescuers by emotionally rescuing us from the villainous Persecutor.

The reality is that the Rescuer is confirming that we (the Victim) are weak, and the situation is beyond our ability to cope with or thrive in. When the drama grows stronger and wider in its impact, any concern over the triggering cause will be swept under the carpet, and the drama will take center stage. You now see the Persecutor (and how they "treated you") as the problem. This allows you (the Victim) to brush aside the issue that brought about the drama in the first place. Once you have stepped into the drama triangle you are avoiding personal responsibility for your own emotional wellbeing, abdicating your personal autonomy, and denying your personal power to choose and maintain boundaries for yourself.

To move up a step, you must accomplish three mental and emotional objectives:

1. You must reject the drama triangle roles. This starts by emotionally owning that you have engaged in the triangle to avoid your internal anxiety over the confronting person or issue. If you were engaging in the drama triangle, you must strive to explain the interactions to yourself without using these categories. You must strive to understand the damage you have done to your own heart, and the damage you tried to do to theirs!
2. You must own the entire *combat*. The entire combative exchange happened when you responded with (took action on) your Judgment mindset. Until then, the relationship was not *combat*; it was *conflict*. The other person was having this conflict over a circumstance, and (in their distress) they invited you to fight with them to distract them from their less-than mental and emotional experience. Until then, the relationship wasn't combat; it was just a person having a bad day. *But* they did stress out; you did judge them as attacking; you did act in response; so, now *you must own all the outcomes*. If you do not own the outcomes, you will not be able to do the next item in this step.
3. You must give restitution. Restitution is paying back something of equal or greater value. If your actions damaged respect, then you must give respect. If your actions and words created pain, you must give

comfort. Generally, people don't go far enough with restitution. If you look at ancient societal codes like the laws of Moses (Exodus 21 and Leviticus 6) or Hammurabi, you will find that the prescribed payback is about 133% (averaged across all categories). People need replacement for their loss, but they don't feel made whole until their pain and suffering gets compensation. This means that if you verbally fought with the person for an hour, your restitution should be more than saying, "Sorry." Your payback should take longer, be more public, and become more pronounced!

REMINDER: These things must also be done *emotionally*! And *don't* forget the Rescuers! If you defaced someone's reputation to get rescued, then you must just as publicly repair their reputation with the Rescuers! Doing this work moves you up *only one step*. Then, you must do the work to move above the Judgment Step.

If you don't do the work to move up a step, then your fight with the person will grow in firmness of perception and may grow to a point where the original offense becomes obscured. This will make the offense more difficult to resolve. The momentary feeling of being less-than can become an "I can't" conviction that you come to believe about yourself. This becomes an ongoing pain that can spread to other relationships. Therefore, people relating at this level can easily devolve another step into separation and avoidance.

Step Three (Going Down) Is Labeled the **Separation** Step

When you stand on the Separation Step, your mindset toward the other person is to disassociate and avoid. Your experience is that you have been attacked so painfully or repeatedly (or both) that you prefer to avoid any kind of interaction with that person. Your expectation is that you will not get anything good out of this situation, so you just try to go around or go away from the person to find satisfaction for yourself.

You may even think: "I never wanted the relationship to be like this." But you will see that as the other person's fault. This is a resignation mindset, or a mindset characterized by burning anger and hopeless despair, and this mindset is often accompanied by depression. In this mental and emotional position, we isolate ourselves to preserve some limited happiness.

To move up a step, you must accomplish three mental and emotional objectives:

1. You must reject anger, combativeness, and war and you must accept inner peace, security, and the sense of well-being that comes with personal responsibility and self-ownership! You may have made a mess of things in yourself and in other's lives but you are still due the self-respect and peace due to any person.
2. You must reject the idea that you are going to "do this for that." In other words, you must reject the *transactional* idea concerning emotional engagement and accept the idea that you can *choose* your emotional state apart from the circumstances and people in your life. You must reject cause and effect thinking and accept choice as the basis for your emotional life. You must accept that *you* can choose who *you* desire to be.
3. You must reengage life to find happiness. If necessary, you must reengage with past hurtful people to resolve personal problems and move up the steps. While you can have counselors help you, in the end *you* must choose to pursue health and bell-being for your own sake.

REMINDER: These things must also be done *emotionally*! The pursuit of health and well-being *does not require you to endanger yourself physically*. Many emotionally abusive relationships become physically abusive as well. If you must clear the air (move up the steps) with someone who has been unsafe physically before, be sure to do it in such a way as you do not put yourself in current danger!

Also, *don't* expect others to proceed up the lower steps *with you*. This is your escape from your dungeon that you put yourself in, and **your escape does not require their participation**. These basement-dwelling relationships can even be escaped when the other person has died! Climbing the lowers steps is personal not interpersonal, even though some of the work can be done in an interpersonal manner.

Figure 3: Anchors Stop Movement

If you don't do the work to move *up* a step, then your struggle with the person will grow into a fixed place of hardness and pain in your life that hardens you against desires for better things relationally and emotionally.

This sad state becomes a *boat anchor* to your hopes and dreams for yourself. No matter how much sail you desire to put up to move your life away from this port of pain, your boat will not move, and you will tend to bring other relationships to the same end. That creates more and more anchors. Unresolved emotional turmoil keeps people from moving up the steps to better things relationally. Moving up the steps is only sure way I have seen people free themselves for the pain of their relational past.

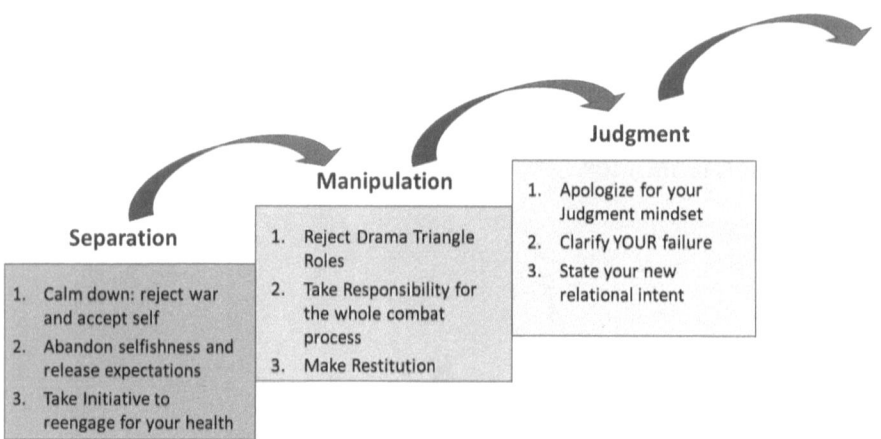

Figure 4: Moving Past the Past

Ground Floor – How It Works

We have covered the three descending steps into relational-emotional separation, and later we will be covering the ascending three steps of relational-emotional growth into unity. Now we are going to look at the most important split second of emotional bonding at any level: the split second when you are confronted by something outside your emotional expectations for that relationship. This is a moment where you have the power to suspend perception, a fraction of a second where you can stop the mind games and reject preconceived perceptions.

Consider this scenario: you are in a relationship on the Manipulation Step. Due to this position, you will naturally perceive the other person's actions as negative or manipulative toward you. You will believe their words and actions exist *for their best interest without consideration of the impact on you.* You will effectively engage in the Karpman Drama Triangle (as a Victim, Persecutor, or Rescuer) in an attempt to survive the situation because you perceive it to be an attack on your well-being or mental-emotional autonomy. *But* when confronted by something *outside* these negative emotional assumptions, you could believe differently.

This opportunity exists during a split second. In that moment you will either suspend your preexisting perceptions and judgments about the other person, or you will give in to the emotional assumptions of the Manipulation Step.

Example: A young wife (Ellen) stands on the Manipulation Step with her mother-in-law (Sue). It seems to Ellen that Sue hates everything she does to be a supportive wife and mother. Ellen sees her mother-in-law as critical about everything and invasive with her opinions. Then, Ellen hears from her sister-in-law Stacey about how much she hates being on the losing end when Sue compares Stacy to Ellen! Ellen hears that Sue presents Ellen to Stacey as an excellent wife and mother, and Stacey is always left feeling less than Ellen.

In this moment, Ellen realizes she has been *praised* by someone by whom she *expected to be criticized*. This report from Stacy comes from *outside* the framework of Ellen's expectations within the Manipulation Step. What will she believe?

- Ellen could see Sue as manipulating Stacey—this will require *no work* emotionally—and this is the typical choice for those on the Manipulation Step.
- Ellen could suspend her judgment, reject the assumptions inherent in the Manipulation Step, and believe something more positive about Sue.

Ellen could:

- Believe Sue is just a person who wants to give her family the benefit of her life experience but is awkward about it; or
- Believe Sue is misunderstood by Stacey and perhaps even by herself; or
- Believe Stacey and Ellen have been interpreting Sue as critical (due to insecurities within themselves) when Sue is actually trying to be helpful.

These more emotionally open thoughts allow Ellen to have choices that the Manipulation Step does not! Ellen could now choose to:

- Offer comfort to Stacey that does not involve Ellen as the emotional Rescuer in the Karpman Drama Triangle.
- Challenge Stacey and herself to be more accepting of Sue's opinions by seeing her words as helpful-in-intent, regardless of the delivery.
- Work on the triggers that cause her to interpret others as attacking when they don't have to be interpreted that way.
- Work on being a peacemaker by overlooking possible petty motives and offering olive-branch responses that both express less combative or guarded emotions and are more emotionally hopeful and warm.

Perceptions about actions and words can be resisted or suspended momentarily so that we can consider other possible interpretations. During those suspended moments, we can consider what we really believe (or desire to believe) about the other person. Having considered these options, we can *choose*. This choice will push us up a step or take us down a step.

When your actions **DON'T** meet
my expectations?
What will I do?

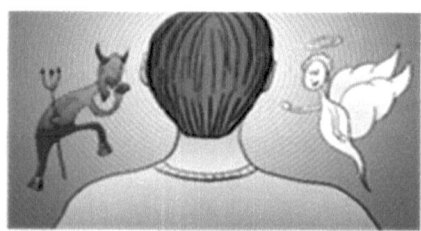

Will I suspend my reaction and
consider something better?

Figure 5: Choice Moments — Reaction or Reflection

Because we ***can*** suspend reactions this makes our action (to pause and consider, or not) a *choice.* Subsequently, we are responsible for ***our*** *relational-emotional condition* concerning every person we relate to, even those who physically victimize us.

If the history of human relations has taught us anything, it is that regardless of the circumstantial actions or the intentions behind the actions of others, *your* mental-emotional well-being is formed by *your* choices. Many prisoners of war and abuse victims have emotionally freed themselves from their abusers to live emotionally healthy lives.

Such was the outcome for Corrie Ten Boom. Ten Boom survived the Nazi concentration camp at Ravensbrück, and she faced the man who murdered her sister and friends twenty years after her physical freedom was secured by soldiers. Through this unexpected encounter, Ten Boom realized: She was free from her emotional burden. She could openly forgive the murderer. And she remained at peace in her soul concerning him.

These stories teach us that we have the ability to influence and control our mental well-being. But we do have to suspend our negative perceptions and open ourselves up to belief in something greater for ourselves and our lives.

As we mentioned when talking about the lower steps, objective judgment is a myth. (The best we can humanly produce are collective probabilities and assumptions.) Neither Ellen nor Stacey can objectively *know with certainty* the intent behind Sue's actions and words. The only person who could know (to some degree) is Sue. Since intent must be ***expressed*** to you and ***believed*** by you; why doesn't Sue or Ellen just *ask* about intent? What stops them from considering and believing better things? Why do people find it so hard to believe in ourselves and others? Why do we give in to negative interpretations when circumstances appear to be contrary to our own well-being, hopes, and desires?

What will you do during the split seconds in your relationships? What you do in your relationships during those split seconds determines: your relational satisfaction, emotional health, and well-being. Those split-second responses can lead to a life filled with abundance and blessing.

But by failing to believe in other people, you can close the door to these outcomes. That negative response leaves you running, hiding, conniving, struggling, fighting, and manipulating to achieve a substandard entitlement to ever-increasing, unmet desires. While your appetite for more grows, your satisfaction with what you gain shrinks. You realize less and less abundance, no matter how much you have. Those who reject hope and choose to struggle against others live lonely, empty lives that are susceptible to life's harsh realities without support or comfort.

So, remember this truth: Regardless of the difficulty in the struggle, there is more to be gained in unity than will be lost in trying to make it happen.

Moving Up the Stairs

Getting out of the basement is an individual journey, but advancements toward unity are taken together with others. Those who join to reach unity experience freedom and excitement. We will start with the lower step toward unity called the Innocence Step and describe the progression through the Cooperation Step and on into the Empowerment Step. These relationships make up *all* our positive energizing relationships! None of these relationships function by way of either compulsion or coercion.

The goal of reading through these descriptions is to allow you to place your *you-are-here* dot on the map! So, to place your dot, think of some relationship and start reading! The following three steps describe an ever-increasing ascent into emotional unity.

Step One (Going Up) Is Labeled the **Innocence** Step

Freedom to engage or disengage according to what you freely agree to for the sake of your own satisfaction is the hallmark of this step! There is no obligation except those you agree to! These are relationships that you engage in that will vary in importance but not in either expectation or accountability. These relationships can span quite a spectrum when it comes to affinity or closeness. They might be:

- **An acquaintance**, a person you might recognize and know something about (but only through hearsay or direct observation) and might have some level of physical interaction with. *Examples: grocery store clerk, mailman, neighbor that you don't relate to, the package delivery man, a cousin that you have never actually met.*
- **A casual relationship**, one *that you don't seek out* with a person whose actions don't impact your life physically. The interactions that you have are because your life crosses paths with theirs. You intentionally share nothing of emotional consequence because you are not inviting the person closer to you, although you might talk about mundane life situations such as the news, weather, or sports. *Examples: a friend, a friend's friend, a distant relative met at a reunion, a former classmate, a former fellow-employee, and such.*

To keep these relationships healthy *and at this level*, certain disciplines must be engaged. The disciplines are relational habits that keep the relationships vital but also keep them at the Innocence Step.

Relational Drift can happen when these habits are not maintained, and relationships can become confusing, prone to misunderstanding, and open to hurtful interpretation of your actions. To grow the relationship beyond the Innocence Step you would need to create a mutual desire to move the relationship forward and start practicing the disciplines and habits appropriate for the next step. But to keep these casual relationships **healthy and keep them at this step,** begin building the following habits:

1. **Listen and speak to their concerns *first*.** Listening is a dying art, but listening is critical to this relational

step. People talk about stuff; it's part of what makes them friends. But when we don't make listening the focus, and we start talking too soon—or worse we respond to their concerns with our concerns—we are priming the system for conflict. Practice reflective listening, listening to clarify and understand the other person's issue. Asking questions to facilitate their understanding and self-acceptance is the best habit to build friendships at this step. When we interject our perspectives, we start shaping theirs without permission, and these relationships are not strong enough to endure that. When you have brought a person (through active questions and listening) to a new perspective on themselves and their issues, *then* you *might* gain the invitation to give an opinion. Until then, talk less and listen more.
2. **Be sensitive to triggering issues.** Sooner or later, you will find their sensitive issues, and the best practice is to let sleeping dogs lie. Don't poke the bear and incite people to be out of control when you know they have a self-control issue. This could be anything from your friend is an alcoholic (so don't offer them a beer) to you friend is an ardent sports fan for a specific team (so don't discuss how they lost the last game). If you do run aground on a sensitivity issue, *let it go*. Don't keep doing it!
3. **Don't try to support yourself through these relationships.** These relationships are for satisfaction, interest, and enjoyment; do not encumber them with life's weightier issues or invite them to share the burden of your life's responsibilities. Don't ask your friend to watch your dog when you go out of town! It is just such innocently offered and accepted responsibilities that begin to erode the boundaries of these relationships. What does it do to the relationship when the person accepts this responsibility? It begins the process of inviting the person to deeper commentary and involvement in your life. Suddenly,

your friend is giving you their opinion on how you live your life. Or worse, something happens to the dog, and the friendship is damaged by disappointment and pain. That is not what these relationships are for!

Step Two (Going Up) is Labeled the **Cooperation** Step

Action has been added to the relationship, and the relationship must grow to support it! The other person's actions now directly impact your life-satisfaction. Shared responsibility and ownership of a common goal is a defining characteristic of this step! An obligation exists because you have discussed expectations, and an agreement was reached! Now, the promise you made to act in collaboration together has created the opportunity for either satisfaction or disappointment. This opportunity will impact each person's satisfaction and thus their relationship. These relationships can vary in emotional connection, but they work the same concerning expectation and accountability. If you work for someone (and most people do), you should be aware that most employment relationships are based in this step. These relationships might be:

- **A connected relationship.** This relationship involves a person whose actions and performance directly impact your life physically and with whom you have regular interaction. If the person left the relationship, they would probably be replaced, not pursued. The nature of your conversation will include tactical, informational content concerning shared activity and might include non-sensitive relational content. You probably know something about the person on an emotional level, but you don't seek them out for emotional sharing. Some limited sharing of resources (time, energy, and money) might happen. *Examples: Casual friends, advisors, coworkers, some family members, personal service people (nurse, doctor, therapist, aid, assistant, and such), the person who mows your lawn, a neighbor with whom you talk about* *neighborhood things, many people in a small town or village.*

- **A close relationship**. This relationship involves a person you intentionally pursued for relationship and with whom you are willing to be transparent and vulnerable up to certain boundaries. Life resources are freely shared but purposefully kept in balance. You know them through specific times of sharing and vulnerability. *Example: Friends, most siblings and family members, romantic relationships, and such.*

Again, to grow the relationship beyond this step you would need to create a mutually accepted bond and start practicing the disciplines and habits of the next step. But to keep such relationships **healthy and keep them on this Step**, begin building the following habits:

1. **Maintain respectful candor.** Speak the truth, but do so in a way that is respectful in demeanor and respectful of the other person's autonomy. These relationships are freely entered and are best maintained when that freedom to engage is respected and preserved. This will not be true if people are hiding the truth from each other, even when the intent is to preserve emotional connection. Emotional connections preserved through limited truthfulness are emotionally manipulative, and thus the bond is falsely perceived.

2. **Refine role and commitments.** A trademark conversation for this level of relationship is a boundary-defining conversation that produces expectations and accountability around either task performance or the use of personal resources. These exchanges must occur without coercion or leverage. A freely given yes is a platform for future conversations about accountability, and such a response must therefore be entered freely if the future accountability is also to go well.

3. **Invest relationally through the Bonding Triangle.** The Bonding Triangle is the opposite of the Drama Triangle in that you are always accountable for yourself!

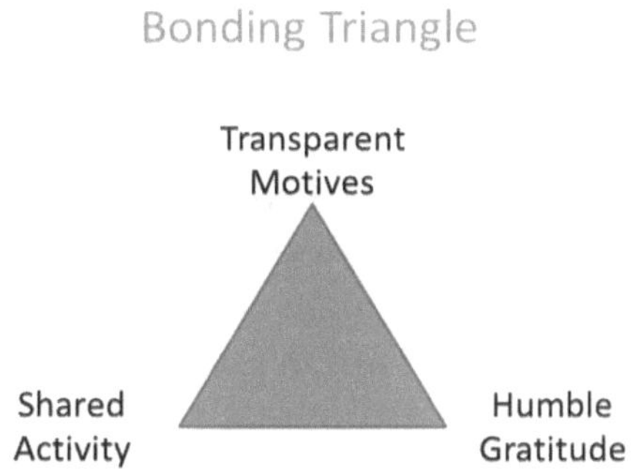

Bonding Triangle

Transparent Motives

Shared Activity

Humble Gratitude

Figure 6: The Bonding Triangle

Core to the idea of self-acceptance is the concept of *autonomous value production*. That phrase means you have the power to produce something of value as a human being. The points of the Bonding Triangle represent three different types of contribution that you bring to your relationships to help the people build the groundwork of trust.

  a. **Transparent motives.** If you are a mature adult living within a relational community, you will be working on aligning your motives to the community's acceptable boundaries. As such, you are free to share your motives without either a sense of loss or a fear of reprisal because the community accepts the idea that all people have self-interest and motive. The community also accepts that these motives are appropriate to be shared within the community or group. All free societies accept the first principle from chapter one: Relationships are about personal satisfaction; it's all about you.

b. **Shared activity**. All people living in a community have some ability to help the community thrive. When you share that ability profitably, you help others accept that you are (to some degree) entrusting your satisfaction to the group's accomplishments. This helps them interpret your actions as trustworthy and helps develop a positive bond.
  c. **Humble gratitude**. This might be the most critical element because the struggle-to-achieve is a more common human condition than achievement itself. When you are in the achievement process, how you respond attitudinally—concerning expressions of gratefulness and honor to all parties of the community—is interpersonally revealing. Cronyism, judgment, pride, arrogance, entitlement, self-aggrandizement, and self-promotion all display a lack of humility that devastates the group's trust. Regular expressions of humility and gratitude build a strong foundation for interpersonal trust and bonding.

Step Three (Going Up) Is Labeled the **Empowerment** Step

When action is added to a relationship, and the relationship grows strong to support it, there is yet another higher form of relational expectation. This level of relational bond is often referred to as leadership, but we have named it Empowerment for its primary attitude (like the other steps). Empowerment means *your* concern has become that the *other person* experiences greater levels of freedom and ability to act for the good of the whole and that these actions would yield greater fruit. These relationships might be:

- **A connected relationship.** This involves a person whose actions and performance directly impact your life physically and with whom you have repeated or regular interaction. If the person left the relationship, they would probably be replaced, not pursued. The nature of your conversation will include tactical, informational content concerning shared activity and might include non-sensitive relational content. You probably know something about the person on an emotional level, but you don't seek them out for emotional sharing. Some limited sharing of resources (time, energy, and money) might happen. *Examples: Casual friends, advisors, coworkers, some family members, personal service people (nurse, doctor, therapist, aid, or assistant) the person who mows your lawn, a neighbor with whom you talk about neighborhood things, many people in a small town or village.*

- **A close relationship.** This involves a person who is intentionally pursued for relationship and with whom you are willing to be transparent and vulnerable up to certain boundaries. Life resources are freely shared but purposefully kept in balance. You know them through specific times of sharing and vulnerability. *Example: friends, most siblings and family members, romantic relationships, and such.*

- **An intimate relationship.** This involves a person who knows you well enough to correct your self-perceptions. These relationships have access to your time, energy, and money in an unguarded, non-transactional manner because you trust them not to violate your boundaries or your best interest. *Example: parent, spouse, some siblings, and such.*

Perhaps the most widely known and accepted version of a relationship on the Empowerment Step is found in both marriage and parenting. However, upon closer inspection, we find people stepping up to Empowerment in many places. In organizations with empowering leadership, we can often find the same principles in action. To **maintain a healthy relationship at this step** we must engage in *all* the former disciplines described above and three others:

1. **Endure hardship for the future.** If you are going to build a bond where you go beyond the transactional agreements and lead, and others feel free to follow and give without thought of reciprocation, you are going to have to sacrifice (to some degree) satisfaction in the present for the sake of future desired state. You will need to endure hardship. [Leaders are hardy, single-minded, and driven people. They are willing to sacrifice for their dreams and for their people.] This requires you to treat people not just according to their current actions (as in the Cooperation Step) but also according to their future potential.

2. **Be others-centered**. To build bonds at this level you need to understand people and show understanding in your treatment of them. You will need to burden yourself with a sense of responsibility for their motivations and satisfaction. Your *motive* must become concern for their well-being. In combination with the futurist outlook, this means treating people with an awareness of their future well-being. In other words, you must treat them in accordance with their fullest human potential.

3. **Increase open one-mindedness**. Much has been said about diversity of thought within leadership relationships, but what those authors are mostly talking about is acceptance of divergent thought. *But* while the acceptance (openness) toward divergent thought is a core part of a leader's relationship to others, such acceptance only supports the leader's one-mindedness. Those following you must agree and commit to *your* mindset on the organization, group, or relationship's intentions and goals. So, increasing the number and scope of one-minded (unified) thoughts, feelings, and actions—while still providing openness toward divergence—is a primary discipline for empowering relationships.

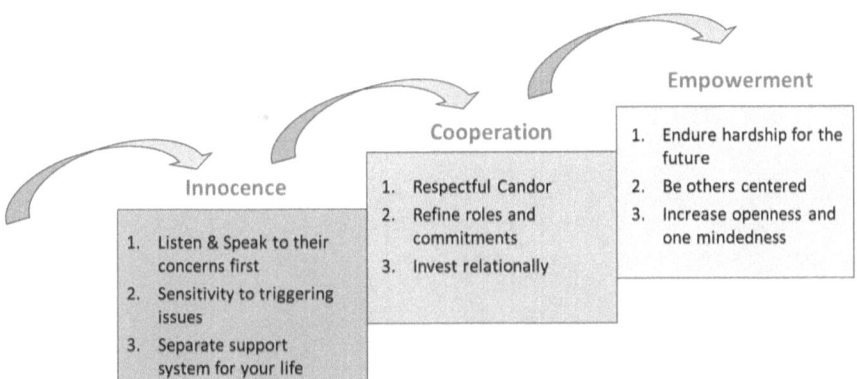

Figure 7: Moving toward Unity

Every relationship you have stands somewhere on the relational steps. The amount of relational stress you have is usually connected to the number of relationships that are changing by shifting up and down the steps. Keeping relationships on the same step reduces relational stress. Yet each engagement either reinforces or confronts the essence of the step we believe the relationship to be on. So, when you conform your actions to the essence of each step, you experience less change and less stress; your *actions* create your relational truth. In this model you don't have to live tomorrow with today's thoughts and emotions, but your *actions* carry on and create the circumstances for your relationships in the future.

Chapter THREE – Becoming a Good "First Responder"

Part 1 — Three Lies and Six Practices That Will Always Be in Your Way

While each relational step has its own stabilizing or strengthening disciplines, each relational event has three common and very important experiential-moments. When our first response in these three moments meets the other person's positive relational expectations, the person is *far more likely* to summarize the event in a positive bond-building way. And they are also far more likely to provide a reciprocal relational experience that builds the relationship, community commitments, and organizational outcomes.

To better understand and produce positive results in these critical relationship-forming moments, we will first look at six expressions that deeply impact people. For these expressions to produce the bond-shaping impact we desire, they must be delivered as your instinctive *first response* during the critical moment. After reading the description for each skill, it would be wise to see how well you can deliver this response by standing in front of a mirror and practicing.

To do this well, you need to do away with three twisted ideas about relationships that are currently confusing our world. And you will need to replace them with sound relational truth.

Falsehood #1. Your *instinctive* first response to a relational event represents your true self. To consciously alter it in any way produces a "fake you" and makes honest relationship impossible.

Truth #1. You can choose both instinctive and self-controlled responses to your life's relational events. Using the response that produces the best good for your relationship reveals your character, love for others, self-respect, and self-discipline.

Therefore, you will *never* be wrong to present what is in the best interest of the other person to create a bond with them rather than expressing yourself in an uncontrolled, instinctive manner in the name of authentic self-expression. To do otherwise will harm others.

Falsehood #2. To maximize your potential satisfaction in this life, the good for self must be prioritized above the good for others. To prioritize them otherwise is to subjugate yourself to others who will inhibit your potential, expose you to abuse, and leverage your abilities to their benefit. The individual, not the community, contains the potential and realizes the greatest results.

Truth #2. To maximize your satisfaction in this life, what benefits relational unity must be prioritized above what benefits your self-expression. To prioritize them otherwise fails to build a support community to maximize your potential, protect your self-imposed limitations, and leverage their abilities to your benefit. The community, not the individual, contains the greatest potential and realizes the greatest results.

Therefore, putting the good of the whole before the good of the one always produces greater results, because it produces the best for both oneself and for all the others, too. There is no human way to be totally selfless, nor is there a way to be totally self-reliant. We thrive in community. To take actions apart from any concern for others will destroy the whole (including ourselves), and to take actions without concern for the one weakens and destroys the whole in that it is now missing the potential to be gained from the part.

Falsehood #3. Humanity's amassed resources (time, talent, things) are greater than or equal to what *you* need. So—from a relational viewpoint and generally in life—you must *take* what you need to *get* what you want.

Truth #3. Humanity's amassed resources (time, talent, things) are less than or equal to what *all* people need. So—from a relational viewpoint and generally in life—you must *give* what you have to *get* what you want.

So, to actively *produce* time, talent, and things and to contribute them to the common good ultimately provides the path to your greatest satisfaction. You *do* have the ability to do what is needed if you desire to give. Conversely, you never give that which you believe you don't have.

So, yes, I am advocating for three very old-fashioned ideas:

- Placing the collective good above your own personal desire,
- Giving (even sacrificially so) to receive, and
- Speaking that intends to impact others well rather than to express oneself fully.

Call me old-fashioned, but these are time-tested and generationally proven concepts for relational connection. You will have heard some version of "Personal growth comes through pain, suffering, struggling, and strife" but the truth is personal growth comes through overcoming those things and reaching a place of truth, unity, and peace. Therefore, I believe your best chance at healthy, intimate relationships finds a home in an atmosphere of peace supported by these ideals not friction and warfare.

Let's look at a list of things that rarely help anyone who is trying to reach peace. Expressions such as:

- **Hundreds** — Terms like *always* and *never* convey a 100% all-in, all-out perspective and an inflexibility concerning the issues.

- **Explosives** — Emotions add energy to discussion when trying to bring about a conviction everyone can collectively support; things like crying, accusing, and shouting don't help.
- **Labels** — This is also not helpful. Stick to discussing specific observable behaviors and actions that were taken in this event, not the categories and labels often used for those words and actions.
- **Mind Reading** — *You* don't know for certain other people's intent and motives. You only know your observations of their actions and expressions. Telling another person what they intended, thought, or felt (no matter what your evidence might be) puts you on shaky ground and can reignite combat. Most of the time, people don't even know the fulness of their own motivations, let alone someone else's.
- **Expansion** – When struggling with someone of this type. Stay on target and try to keep them on the target. The target is a path forward that everyone can commit to.
- **Threats** — This seem obvious, but it's not. In the attempt to convey consequences or cause-and-effect concerning choices, these comments can often be taken as threats. The removal of a person's right or ability to choose provides the core element that makes a statement into a threat. So, make statements that clarify the scope and autonomy for decision making.

Figure 8: Helmets Are for Warfare

These are all inflammatory responses more accustomed to create warfare than to reduce it. If we are going to be the first responders in any relational crisis (including our own), then we must be able to create peace so that intimacy and connection can flourish.

Part 2: Six First-Response Skills We Need to Master

Each of the following expressions is designed to engage a specific part of the human mind. The human mind has six way of perceiving or interpreting the input from our body (brain). So, the mind has these six perceptive modes, and each of them thirsts for satisfaction and drives our decisions toward satisfaction. We all have these perceptive modes, but they are not all equally strong. They do not have the same order of prioritization, the sequence of urgency for satisfaction.

The Process Communication Model discovered by Dr. Taibi Kahler outlines these thirsts and refers to them as personality types. Each type has highly correlated communication methods and psychological needs. The Six Expressions will work best when used to understand people who center their psychological outlook around that particular function or perception.

Expression #1: Relaxed Humor

Figure 9: Relaxed Humor
People Type: Rebel

The Rebel is the part of the human psyche that produces your *current preferences*, and for 20% of the population this is their strongest (base) perception. Statistically, this 20% is 60% female and 40% male. The person living out of their Rebel is not necessarily a rebellious person! They are a joy-based or enjoyment-based person. This part of the psyche has *strong* like-or-dislike reactions (preference reactions) to stimuli.

People whose psyche is based in this function have dramatic preference reactions to everything, and this is their basis for processing the world around them. Some of their common traits are being: fun-loving, playful, physically demonstrative, expressively exaggerated, and mood oriented. When these people are happy, it is unacceptable for you to be sad. When these people are sad, it is unacceptable for you to be happy, and they will work to make it so!

Rebels perceive the world through the lens of like and want, and their corresponding superpowers are their ability to understand and express what people (including themselves) really *want* and to influence other people's mood with their own. They want a world where each person is free to "be themselves" (pursue their desires) without being burdened by limits or others.

Anxiety Pathway for the REBEL

When they are not experiencing the world they prefer, the Rebel will attempt to tell you what they want, but it will often sound whiny. They may often complain because you are making it difficult for them to feel free to pursue what they want. When anxiety increases, their whining about circumstances will turn to outright blaming their lack of happiness (or goal accomplishment) on others or the circumstances created by others. They may even invent the circumstances! They will present others as having ruined their happiness or achievement; they will blame their circumstance on people or things other than themselves.

Because they see others as "being mean to them," they feel justified in demonstrating just how monstrous people can be. As they fall into third-degree distress, they will provoke you to a point that you censure them with uncontrolled actions. This proves *to them* that you are a mean, miserable, unhappy person who wants to make them unhappy.

Facing Responsibility — Why It Works

The response of Relaxed Humor is disarming and puts personal responsibility in proper perspective. Until time travel becomes possible, anything that has happened cannot be undone. Trying to assign blame is a basically fruitless exercise because afterwards we still have the issue to resolve.

Relaxed Humor put this behavior into perspective. It prioritizes human acceptance above human drama and makes light of the human condition. For those well practiced, Relaxed Humor can be done with sensitivity to human struggle. This relaxed or laid-back expression releases the Rebel from feeling that they are responsible for others' happiness, and being humorous makes their social obligations and responsibilities less burdensome.

In the Mirror:

Act out a scene where people are intense or whiny while they shift blame and dodge accountability. Produce a lax or fluid posture. Sit with an open body posture, relax your shoulders, lean back from others, and say something funny with a laid-back or light-hearted tone of voice. Use humorous words from movies, songs, and pop culture to remind everyone that this event is not unique to the human condition; it is not likely to end the world. Do so without being intense or serious in your presentation.

Expression #2 Respectful Conviction

Figure 10: Respectful Conviction

People Type: – Persister

The Persister is the part of the human psyche that produces your willfulness (force of will, level of commitment, and conviction), and for 10% of the population this is their strongest (base) perception. Statistically, this 10% is 75% male and 25% female. The Persister is committed to every thought and action that they produce. This deliberateness expresses itself as both opinion and judgment concerning all life stimuli. The value of all things is determined by its enablement for the current trajectory of their will. They judge the value of one thing against another at blazing speed and speak that judgment with confidence and conviction, regardless of its accuracy. They care little whether their judgment helps the common good or whether they have used thoroughness during the formation of their perspective. Their superpower is their ability to hold to a course of action no matter what the personal repercussions. Is it any surprise that most of our presidents, judges, police officers, and career military personnel have been Persister personalities?

Anxiety Pathway for the PERSISTER

When the Persister comes across stimuli that are unexpected or at first blush are not aligned to their current trajectory, they experience anxiety. This will often cause them to lump such stimuli in with all the other things in life that resist their convictions. The proverbial glass is now half empty, and they will tend to verbalize their negative critique without expressing any positives. If disrespect for their perspective is voiced, or agreement is not readily expressed, they can go into second-degree distress.

The Persister in such distress will double down on their opinion and become more critical, condemning, and aggressive in their presentation to cover their unacknowledged fear that their position might fail to help the other person. They will tend to polarize perspectives to win others over and will condemn the character of those who believe otherwise.

Tension will increase when they descend into third-degree distress, and they may forsake others as irredeemable! In their mind, they justify their harshness with the thought that they tried to help but the other person just would not commit to what was best, which is always defined by the Persister's viewpoint!

Facing Fear with Respectful Conviction — Why It Works

The Persister lives in a near constant state of all-in commitment to everything that they believe. This makes even the smallest resistance a cause for concern. The response of Respectful Conviction is disarming and puts personal fears and concerns into proper perspective. While what is best for all *can* be determined, the response that mixes respect for the Persister's authority and validation for the good their conviction has produced historically will de-escalate tension and create openness.

Respectful conviction often calms the situation because it refocuses the person on their opinion instead of their feeling offense that the other person does not share it. Respectful acknowledgement of the Persister validates their fears and their unacknowledged desire to protect the other person with the Persister's value system. This will lead them to a point where their conviction scales back down to their actual scope of authority.

Asking questions is the best way to lead a Persister to a conviction that they can hold to—or the conditions under which they might—while they attempt to help the other person. Asking questions helps the Persister find this revised conviction, so they don't just throw up their hands and forsake the other person. Respectful acknowledgement for the value of Persisters, their resources, and their relationships, can only ease their fears and can bring about peace, or at least a cease-fire.

In the Mirror

Act out a scene where people are intense and judgmental and in which people are angry and pointing accusingly at one another. Produce a calm, commanding, self-controlled, and self-reliant, upright posture, who will sit up or stand with feet shoulder-width apart. Let the advocate speak in a clear, firm way concerning their personal level of conviction on the issue. Ask for the Persister to express their opinion in a similar way. Don't fear this because they are going to tell you anyway; you might as well invite them to do it. The advocate can also convey calm and respectful self-possession by not using large or complex terms when small words will do.

Once you have repeated back to the Persister what they are willing to commit to and you have respectfully acknowledged that you are willing to accept *their* terms for *their* actions, then the tension level should be reduced.

Expression #3 Relational Warmth

Figure 11: Relational Warmth

People Type: – Harmonizer

The Harmonizer is the part of the human psyche that produces your ability to feel emotions, and for 30% of the population this is their strongest (base) perception. Statistically, this 30% is 75% female and 25% male. The Harmonizer is feeling their way through life. Their emotions determine what is best to do. What is best is therefore what creates the most emotional connection and closeness around them. Not all their feelings are warm and connection-oriented. With emotion as their strongest ability, emotion also acts as their strongest weapon. Their anger can burn like an active volcano for years, and their disassociation can be like an arctic wind. Their love and affections are intense enough to be legendary.

The Harmonizer's emotional connections are so strong that it seems to weld them to the emotions of others with great perception and fidelity. This is so pronounced that their decisions are often just as influenced by how *they* feel as they are by how the action will likely cause *others* to feel. This type of group processing is so broad that it encompasses the whole crowd and produces a sense of social etiquette or emotional rules designed to protect everyone's emotional state. Their superpowers are compassion and attractional warmth. People seek them for this balm of healing and safety, and it forms the basis of their influence.

Anxiety Pathway for the HARMONIZER

When the Harmonizer comes across stimuli that are perceived as harsh, unkind, or that (at first blush) are not aligned to their feeling toward the person or situation, they experience anxiety. This will often cause them to feel sad. Someone once told me, "Sad and mad are two sides to the same coin, and the coin is a sense of injustice."

The Harmonizer will first try to express that the unfeeling person has gone too far by expressing sadness. Their usually warm, kind look suddenly becomes hesitant and slightly sad looking. When harshness increases or continues, the Harmonizer will drop to second-degree distress and will try to distract the harsh or insensitive person by falsely taking the blame, saying "I'm sorry," and inviting criticism of themselves either to provoke a de-escalation of tension or to provoke warmth and rescue toward them for their undeserved victimhood.

If selflessly throwing themselves on the sacrificial pyre of other people's harsh emotional disregard does not de-escalate the situation—and it doesn't—the Harmonizer will attempt to withdraw. This fails due to the volume of unresolved tension, so in third-degree distress they get rejected.

If the other person will not play this role, the Harmonizer will force them to by expressing so much uncontrolled, intensive, negative emotion about so many random things that the other person backs off and rejects them as irrational. In either case, the Harmonizer's rejection justifies their sense of emotional hurt and abandonment due to what they perceive as a lack of emotional connection in the relationship.

Facing Anger — Why It Works

Nobody likes to see what they look like when they are angry. But being angry for a Harmonizer is deeply self-confronting. Because they want to be warmly connected to everyone and have everyone warmly connected to them, their anger toward people and circumstances confronts their sense of themselves as a kind and loving person. The very awareness the Harmonizer has about their ability to emotionally shred a person contradicts who they desire to be and sets them up for hypocrisy.

Harmonizers hate in response to hate. To ease their inner contradiction, someone must show them relational warmth without regard to how unkind they are being. Not only is relational warmth powerful enough to shock them out of their deepest rages, it is also the lift they seek in each exchange with others. Relational warmth draws out the Harmonizer's very best and provokes their deepest sympathies for others. It disarms their anger with warmth, acceptance, and the relational offer of kindness.

This expression is *very* nonverbal. The content of such speech has only fractional importance compared to the tone of voice, eye contact, and other calming expressions. The only verbal boundaries are around word choice: avoid derogatory, demeaning, or critical words if you want to make a right response.

In the Mirror

Act out a scene where someone is too harsh, emotionally disassociated, or impersonal, and the person you're trying to connect to checks out, takes the blame, apologizes (when they didn't do anything), or invites criticism by criticizing themselves. When your Harmonizer is sacrificing emotionally in any of these ways, either move toward them or show your emotional support for them by using comforting words, soft tones, and calm actions with hands turned palm up. Eye contact and gentle smiles are essential to this expression. The content of any speech has only fractional importance compared to tone of voice, eye contact, and other calming motions.

The only verbal boundaries are around word choice: if you want to make a right response, avoid derogatory, demeaning, or critical words, even if the Harmonizer is saying them.

Expression #4 Reasonable Intellect

Figure 12: Reasonable Intellect

People Type: Thinker

The Thinker is the part of the human psyche that produces your ability to reason (use logic and timing to organize data and action), and for 25% of the population this is their strongest (base) perception. Statistically, this 25% is 75% male and 25% female. The Thinker reasons their way through life. Many Thinkers have internal injunctions against emotion because it tends to cloud logic. Due to this, Thinkers are often unaware of the emotional elements of a situation or problem. This may seem more pronounced in men since the male mind is biologically more prone to compartmentalization.

Do not mistake the ability to reason clearly for the ability to make a decision. Just as often as any other personality type, the Thinker will suspend a decision or procrastinate. They do this because they lack data, want to wait on more information, or because there is too much conflicting data. Sometimes, the data they have can't be logically united to form a clear timeline for events or a clear conclusion to a problem.

As people who are more given to data collection, process control, and logical problem-solving than they are at relational interactions, Thinkers tend to overuse their logic processing in relational situations. The interjection of reason or Q&A into emotional moments, the internal processing of unspoken thoughts, and the insistence on being correct before they take action, can make them seem difficult to get along with at times.

Anxiety Pathway for the THINKER

The Thinker likes to move through life with assurance that they understand the world around them and can with some confidence calculate *the probability of a secure, successful, future state* around their course of action. When the Thinker comes across stimuli that are perceived as incorrect, unvalidated, illogical, or confusing, they will begin to feel anxiety. Anxiety will quickly intensify when these types of stimuli cause a loss of confidence around *the probability of a secure, successful, future state.*

During such a state of agitation, the Thinker will begin to try to think and act for others. They tell themselves things will go better and if they just do it themselves without ever acknowledging how pulling into themselves will affect others and without recognizing their own anxiety.

When the unrecognized anxiety increases, Thinkers look and sound frustrated while inwardly they feel the probable future state that they wanted is slipping away. They will then become argumentative to get others to see reason (their point of view) or acknowledge their perspective. In their final state of distress, Thinkers reject others as unable to think clearly, ignorant, blind to the facts, and stupid.

Reasonable Intellect — Why It Works

Reasoning is the Thinker's superpower, and emotional grief (the limit to reason) is their kryptonite. In the course of life, small losses can be grieved for by simply acknowledging that they have happened, setting the loss aside, and acting with a focus on a new objective. But the emotional loss could be too high a hurdle for the Thinker to get over. I have seen Thinkers express white-knuckled rage over something as simple as their planned restaurant being unexpectedly closed or being three minutes late to an appointment.

The first response of Reasonable Intellect helps the Thinker reestablish a rational outlook and step over the hurdle rather than sinking into their anxiety pathway. Grief makes an emotional adjustment to a circumstance that you would not chose for yourself. While grief makes an emotional adjustment, emotions are biological responses to our thoughts. Thought is the foundation of emotion! Think angry thoughts, and you will feel angry feelings. Therefore, grief has a resolution in thought. Grief rationally requires us to:

- Let go of the investment of emotions and energy lost during the previous path of action.
- Recognize that what has happened is now the new reality (even if the cause is unknowable).
- Build a new focus on a different path of action to readjust our trajectory while recognizing that knowledge (even

perfect knowledge) doesn't protect you or secure your future; it only creates the perception of those things.
- Become positively emotionally settled by recognizing that successful action recreates your perception of security.

In the Mirror:

Act out a scene where the Thinker gets anxious. Speak without expressing emotion: nothing positive, nothing negative. Too much eye contact or voice inflection is bound to create tension or misunderstanding, so these should also be avoided. Your body language should also reflect this calm focus on problem-solving. Ask questions that seek understanding of facts (not opinions, emotions, or conjecture); focus your words on data, logic, timing, and actions. If you persist in this calm deliberation and factual inquiry, the Thinker will tend to see the interaction as positive and will also move away from their inner anxiety.

Expression #5 Reflective Space

Figure 13: Reflective Space

People Type: Imaginer

The Imaginer is the part of the human psyche that produces your ability to be inwardly reflective (to consider things and people as they might be—to imagine things that don't exist). For 10% of the population, this is their strongest (base) perception. Statistically, this 10% is 60% female and 40% male. In the

Imaginer's mind, reflection (consideration and imagination) gets greater attention than does outer reality.

In the same way that the Rebel can sense their individuality, the Imaginer can always sense that their awareness of the world is just a perception that is subject to their interpretation and imagination. Reality is moldable. They regularly recast reality into whatever they wish. While they can feel reality's demands pushing in on them, they give those demands minimal energy while giving their imagination most of their energy and focus.

Anxiety Pathway for the IMAGINER

When the Imaginer must spend too much time interacting with the real world and feels the real world demanding too much of their inner world's energy, they become anxious. This anxiety causes them to pull away from the world by promising whatever is demanded so that they can escape into their inner world. These unmet promises then cause anxiety to reach new levels with greater demands from the Imaginer's outer life.

During second-degree distress, rather than giving empty promises to get others to leave them be, they become unresponsive, silent, and unmoving until the demands stop and the people making the demands go away. In third-degree distress, the Imaginer self-justifies their inaction because the others moved on without them; therefore, they must not have really needed the Imaginer's help. When this become habitual (relationally), others stop making demands and learn to live without engaging the Imaginer. The Imaginer gets left behind without direction.

Reflective Space — Why It Works

Reflective Space is a difficult skill to master because, unlike the other skills, this one has no feedback loop. For all the other skills, when you use the skill there will be visual and auditory clues that it is working. With this skill you will see nothing and hear nothing that tells you Reflective Space is working. You must simply trust that it is. The Imaginer's inner world creates their inner motivations and outward actions through a continuous state of inward interpretive reflection and imaginative creation.

When this process gets overloaded with demands or when demands are made for which there is no reflective or imaginative basis, the Imaginer needs time to process. No action will occur until the reflective basis is created. Inviting the Imaginer to engage with you to rest their mind or refocus themselves is both highly attractive and powerfully positive.

In the Mirror

Act out a situation where the Imaginer checks out, becomes silent, or is flippantly responsive, and then *relax*! Let your shoulders relax. Your body language must demonstrate a non-intensive and accepting posture. Tell the Imaginer to take time to reflect on what has been requested, and then wait for the response.

Whatever time frame you think they need, quadruple it, and then wait again. Don't reengage on the subject until the Imaginer initiates it. If it seems that they have forgotten you, you may remind them that they should still take whatever time that they need and that you are still waiting for them. This message must not come across as pressure or a demand but as a desire for their involvement. With a sense that you are being protective of their inner world, they will be free to imagine a solution or create the basis of imagination for their action.

Expression #6 Responsive Energy

Figure 14: Responsive Energy
People Type: Promoter

The Promoter is the part of the human psyche that produces your ability to aspire (hope or seek greatness), and for 5% of the population this is their strongest (base) perception. Statistically, this 5% is 75% male and 25% female. The Promoter is focused on other people's perception of them rather than their own perception of themselves. To the Promoter, making an impact is more about being seen as great than about being truly superior. Like the Imaginer, the Promoter realizes there is a good deal of perception mixed with reality, in the end. So, from infancy they have been learning how to bend reality in their favor by bending people's interpretations of reality (perceptions) rather than by changing people's reality. To many this seems deceptive or manipulative, and it might be. But we all have a Promoter part, and all you must do to see it is read a résumé or go to a job interview.

As a career human resources professional, I can tell you that no one goes into an interview looking to tell the whole and unvarnished truth about their work history. There is *always* a good deal of positive spin put on things, especially negative things. This ability to put things that are attractive to others out in the open while hiding things that would cause concern is the Promoter's function.

The Promoter in you puts your best foot forward. It is the part of you that puts lipstick on a pig and calls it a beauty because that's what people will accept. The Promoter proclaims the Emperor to have grand new clothes until everyone believes it.

Anxiety Pathway for the PROMOTER

When the Promoter does not sense you have the same level of energy for a subject than they do, they begin to feel anxiety. This lack of energy around the incident causes them to try to change your energy level into one more like their own. By various methods of persuasion, they will attempt to energize you.

If this persuasion fails to increase your energies, they will cast aside you, your ideas, feelings, and such. They will belittle you and be unsupportive to you at an exaggerated level. This grows in intensity until they reach third-degree distress when they separate from you, leaving you with a parting threat of impending doom.

Responsive Energy — Why It Works

Responsive Energy means matching their *energy*, not agreeing with their *position*. If they use disgust to present their view about a traditional viewpoint on something (and you disagree), you must show an equal amount of disgust to present the opposite view! When facing any other kind of personality, this would be seen as a loss of self-control and immaturity, but the Promoter sees it as an esteem-giving clash of equals.

When you engage in this way over small things, bigger more negative conflicts can be avoided. After the clash of equals is accomplished, a more reasonable exchange can be started. But each time more people are added, the battle for superiority will likely be repeated.

In the Mirror

There is not much to do here. You simply match the Promoter's tone of voice, demeanor, word choice, and body posture. You do so not to produce dominance but to take the issue of domination off the table.

Part 3: Three "Critical Scenes" That Need a Right "First Response"

I have had several friends that work in first-responder jobs (police, EMT, firefighter, and such), and they all describe the need to quickly assess and do what is most critical to preserve life and minimize further damage. Being a first responder for relationships works much the same. Because, as explained previously, relationships are formed in moments and memories, there are a few critical moments when our initial response needs to preserve the relationship and minimize any relational damage. Any action taken by us during these moments needs to work for the recipient.

There may not be many of these critical moments during the engagement, but there are going to be at least three: the *greeting*, the *goal moment*, and the *goodbye*. Our positive or negative memory of the event will be guided by how satisfactory these three moments were. When we get these moments right, we tend to remember the entire engagement as good. When these moments pass poorly or without satisfaction, we tend to remember the entire engagement as bad.

This is a "numbers game." Regardless of whether you get the moments right or not, you are going to form a memory. But if you miss the mark more times than you get it right, the memory will not be a positive one.

For example: if you are on the Cooperation Step with a coworker, and he approaches you for a Collaborator engagement and you get the Greeting right, the Goal moment wrong, and the Goodbye moment right, that's 2 out of 3. The engagement will be remembered in a positive light, even though the Goal moment was not satisfactory. Due to this positive score, the parameters of the Cooperation Step have been maintained and the relationship remains stable.

But if the engagement contains four Goal moments, and you get all of them wrong, but you still get the Greeting and Goodbye right, that's 2 out of 7, and the engagement will be remembered negatively. Furthermore, this negative engagement will challenge the parameters of the Cooperation Step, and your coworker will need to suspend his reactions, engage the "Bonding Triangle" mindset, and reinforce it with the appropriate actions, or he will begin to slide downward in his emotional house in relation to you.

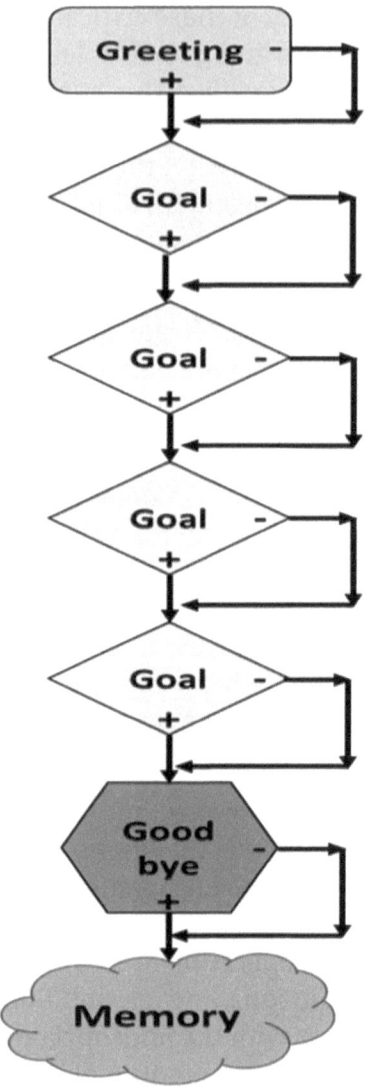

Figure 15: Critical Moments to Memory

Critical Scene #1: Greetings

First-contact moments set the stage for the relational engagement. People who do these moments well tend to be seen as approachable and safe. This helps cement the positive memory for the engagement.

Yet some people will say that all preamble is a waste of time and that first responders should just lead with what they want or just get to the point. I have noticed, however, that the people who say this only say it about people they don't really want to relate to. Further, they are just as hurt or negative in their outlook toward others when they receive no greeting, a cold greeting, or a negative greeting.

The length of the greeting will differ from person to person. It can be as simple as a smile, eye contact, or a hug. Or it could be a 10–15-minute conversation about things other than the purpose of their engagement with you at that moment. In any case, this preconversation connection must be in a form of expression appropriate for the recipient of the greeting. Here are a few examples:

Relaxed Humor: "Hey dude waaaaassssup!"

Respectful Conviction: "Good Morning, I would appreciate getting your perspective on [issue]."

Relational Warmth: "Hi Tom, I heard your son graduated. Congratulations! Did you do anything special?"

Reasonable Intellect: "If you have a few minutes, would you tell me what you know about [topic]."

Reflective Space: A head nod, eye contact, or slight smile may be all that is necessary, although you could just combine that with their name.

Responsive Energy: If they are focused and busy, then go straight to the point with the same attitudes.

- Greeting Moments
    - Set the expectation for the engagement
        - The expectation is *not* that they are going to get what they want, but that the interaction will not be negative.
        - The expectation that they will get what they want by engaging with you is an entitlement attitude, and that is usually a maturity problem.

Critical Scene #2: Goals

As described previously, relationships take place within parameters of expectation (Steps), and you are having regular relational interactions on those steps. Each interaction (according to principle 1) has a purpose. In short, *every* time a person walks up and engages you, they present themselves to you for a reason. In any prolonged engagement with another person there might be several goal moments, each of them must be met with the correct expression. Below are the four reasons people approach and engage others.

Presenting #1: The Closer

Figure 16: A Closer for My Crisis

They want your help. They are engaged in some crisis or situation where your *assistance* is desired to close or complete their situation. These situations could be either simple or complex. The help they need might be knowledge-based, skills-based, or resource-based.

It is important to note that a crisis presentation always includes surrender or submission to you for your help. This aspect of surrender separates the Closer presentation from the others. This is the most common reason why children engage with adults. They want something (justice, an outcome, or a thing) that they can't get by themselves. So, they surrender their life to your influence, so that you can help them achieve what they want.

Closers Done Well:
- Limits to help must be stated immediately.
- The commitment to help must be given (or rejected) as soon as possible.
- The closure of the crisis must be celebrated or recognized.

Presenting #2: The Companion

Figure: 17: A Companion for My Journey

There might be a crisis, *but* the person is not engaging with you for your help, nor do they wish to surrender themselves to you for closure. They just want your companionship while they walk through the situation. There is likely some expectation for emotional, spiritual, or intellectual supportiveness.

This presentation is also used when there is no crisis! Sometimes people engage with you simply because they enjoy your company. This is a very common presentation for peers and friends.

Companionship Done Well:
- I am for you! I am for you making good choices for your best interest. I'm not your Rescuer because I won't empower the belief that you're a Victim.
- I am with you through the process.
- Both parties should experience some satisfaction, but it does not have to be equal or simultaneous.

Presenting #3: The Collaborator

Figure 18: A Collaborator for My Achievements

This presentation is very easily confused with presentation #1 (The Closer) because there *is* an objective result that is at the center of these engagements. The difference is the person does not surrender themselves to you for the solution so much as they create agreements that drive **both** parties toward the agreed upon objective. This will be the presentation form most often used by coworkers, teams, and people engaged through organizational structures.

Collaboration Done Well:
- Commitments are reviewed; goals and roles are clarified.
- Options around solutions are discussed until Win-Win solutions can be committed to.
- Recourse around failure is defined.

Presenting #4: The Commander

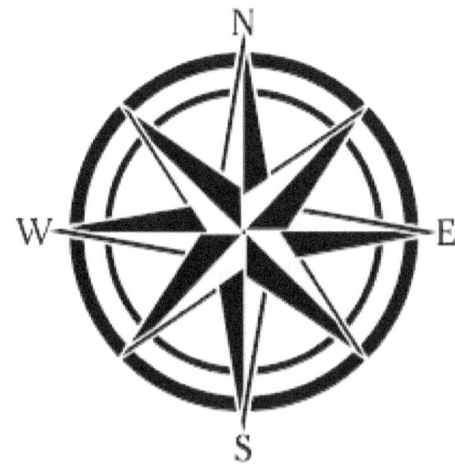

Figure 19: A Commander for My Vision

This presentation is most easily understood as a mixture of presentation #1 (The Closer) and presentation #3 (The Collaborator). There is a common goal or organizational structure holding people together, and then there is a problem. Pastor Bill Hybels said it best, the problem is "Vision Leaks". People turn and engage a Commander because they need someone in whom the vision and direction is clear, sure, and because of their indefatigable energy for the vision; their vision doesn't leak. This could be as simple as a group of friends, trying to decide where to go to dinner, who suddenly turn to the most dominant person and say, "You pick." Or this presentation could be a complex problem faced by an organization that can't be solved without the leader's skills, so the crisis is brought to them. The followers submit to the leader's determination or parameters.

In each case certain things are true: there is a recognized leader-follower relationship, and there is a situation where the follower feels their need to surrender themselves to the leader for the sake of mutual success.

Commander Done Well:
- Necessity of resolution is defined in future-impact terms.
- Ideals are upheld (in word and deed) by the Commander.
- Initiative is recognized, encouraged, and offered by the Commander.

- Goal Moments
  - Satisfies the expectation for the engagement.
    - Whether they were satisfied with what they received or not, the interaction didn't become negative.
    - Because there might be many Goal Moments in a single engagement, using the right expression in each moment can become as much about the number of times you get it right versus how perfectly you do each expression.

Scene 3: Goodbyes

This scene is the anchor point for the result of the engagement with the other person. Goodbyes help us remember the engagement in a positive or negative light by framing the outcome relationally. If greetings help set the tone for the engagement by causing us to remember our relational connection, goodbyes help ground our perspective around the result by putting the result into perspective.

Two people ending a discussion about a painful topic who take the time to reaffirm their relational connection before they disengage from the issue, are far more likely to remember the entire engagement as positive. It is important to see that the goodbye moment is a disengagement moment that may or may not include physical separation. Here are a few examples:

Relaxed Humor – "Hey we got through that diva moment without the snickers!"

Respectful Conviction – "I'm confident you will make it right in the end."

Relational Warmth: "I'm sorry you're having to go through this. Let me know how I can support you."

Reasonable Intellect: "You seem to have done all you can to understand the issue. I think it will work."

Reflective Space: "OK. Seems right."

Responsive Energy If they are excited, be excited; if reserved, show reservedness.

- Goodbye Moments
    - Set the expectation for the next engagement.
        - The expectation is not that the next engagement will go the same as this one ended but that the next engagement will start with at the same level of emotional connection.
        - The expectation may be subject-matter specific.

Part 4: Critical Care (Course Correction)

Sooner or later, you are going to disappoint expectations by not delivering the right expression in the right scene. To speak the right expressions in the right moment all the time takes great wisdom and personal maturity. An incredibly rich and influential king (Solomon of Israel) once had a book of wise sayings put together, and that book contains this saying: "*A word fitly spoken is like apples of gold in settings of silver*" (Proverbs 25:11, English Standard Version*).*

Figure 20: A Word Aptly Spoken

But what about when you miss the mark? How do you fix it? What about when someone misses your mark? How do you fix that?

There is a process for this relational course correction, and it starts with two virtues that are easy to say and hard to gain. The first is **self-awareness**, and the second is **self-control**. Without these virtues your relationships *will* go off the rails and *will not* go the distance.

We are not talking about complete self-awareness or unlimited self-control—just enough to sense something has happened that you did not expect and the ability to stop your visceral, instinctive reaction. *Stop* is a concept that must be taught to humans very early in their psychosocial development, and while it seems simple sounding, many people have never mastered it.

1. Suspend Reaction

For clarity's sake, stop means to become still: cease your current action (including your mouth). Cease your current feelings, thoughts, desires, drives, and hopes. Come to a standstill! Move *out* of the world of reaction and *into* the world of reflection and inquiry. We don't call the first step "stop" because that word also conveys a permanence that this dynamic process does not accept. Relational growth requires you to stop reacting in a relationally destructive way so you can *start* acting in a relationally healthy way. So, we use the phrase "Suspend Reaction" so that you can move back into the world of healthy relational choices.

2. Transparent Expectation

After suspending your internal and external reactions (step 1) you must reveal your inner turmoil to the other person. Before this transparency becomes helpful, you must first *own* your perception of their actions as a perception or observation not as a reality. You must focus on what *you* thought, felt, or did in response to them, not on them.

Having described how the situation impacted you, you *don't* get to prescribe how they should behave in the future. That is how Judgment works. Judgment says I am wronged, and you must do [something] to make it right. Sharing your experience to coerce the other person into living differently is manipulative and will likely create more separation.

During the process of having a transparent conversation around your disappointed expectations, you may find (and should be willing to verbalize) fault in your perception of their actions. If you want this to go well, you must be sure that you don't cross the line by telling or implying that the other person was wrong. You are simply stating that it wasn't what you expected, and it didn't work for you. If the other person expresses sorrow over the current separation and a commitment to move closer to you relationally, you can move to step 3.

3. Vulnerable Aspiration

Becoming vulnerable is difficult in that many people simply don't take it far enough. This conversation does not just reveal what you want physically, intellectually, and emotionally in the here and now. The conversation also includes how you see those thoughts, feelings, and actions culminating to create the shared outcomes for the relationship. Time must be spent here to work toward: common understanding and acceptance of current difficulties, probable limitations, and future desires.

Levels of vulnerability are directly related to security of commitment, relationally. You are not required to be vulnerable with emotionally hurtful or relationally uncommitted people. Expressing aspirations for levels of connection that the relationship is not ready for is a sure way to create emotional withdrawal and separation.

The young woman who shares on your first date her desire to marry you and have three children with you is likely to get nothing she aspires to. In the same way that Transparency of Expectation required a commitment to move closer to the person in a commitment to their well-being, relational health expects a response of reciprocal closeness during conversations about vulnerability.

Reciprocal Concern

Vulnerability shared in the context of relational commitment should result in reciprocal concern about the issue facing the relationship. Concern over the struggle to live together satisfactorily with each other should reach levels that necessitate the pursuit of living for the good of the other person rather than just living for yourself. What is good for the relationship must find a way to be good for the self, and what is good for the self must contribute to the good of the relationship. People have self-interest, and that is healthy, but for relationships to grow, the interest of the one must concern the other to the degree that they can say this is important to both of us. In this reciprocal concern we become one-minded, and a deeper connection is forged.

Chapter FOUR
Four Practice-Accidents

"I want this book to be more like a workshop than and lecture. So, I have put together some stories and questions to help you diagnose and design a repair for a few relational "accidents" to help you practice being a first responder. You would do best to have a group of people who would be willing to do this together so that you could discuss your responses with others.

Story 1: HELP!

Your eight-year-old daughter, Ashley, pours energy into everything she does and is very expressive. When she is happy, it feels like a sunny day, and when she is not happy, she spreads unhappiness like a disease. One day you hear, "Daaaad! Tell bubby [what she calls her brother] to give me my Xbox controller!"

Simultaneous to this, you hear several thumps and thuds, and her brother, Richard, says, "It's not just yours. Stop hitting me!" This is followed by: "She's throwing things!" and "No!"

Suddenly, stomping into the room, Ashley comes to a halt in front of you. Clenched in her little fist is the power cord for the Xbox. Her elbows are locked, chin is tucked in, head is forward, and in a tight, whiny voice she says, "Tell him to give it back!"

What should your First Response be?

Greeting: (☐ Relaxed Humor, ☐ Respectful Conviction, ☐ Relational Warmth, ☐ Reasonable Intellect, ☐ Reflective Space, ☐ Responsive Energy)

Goal: (☐ Closer, ☐ Companion, ☐ Collaborator, ☐ Commander)

Goodbye: (☐ Relaxed Humor, ☐ Respectful Conviction, ☐ Relational Warmth, ☐ Reasonable Intellect, ☐ Reflective Space, ☐ Responsive Energy)

Story 2: The Bad First Date

Ally and David are both thirteen, and while they have been girlfriend and boyfriend before with others, it was really in name only. They spent little to no time alone with the other people. David asked if Ally would be his girlfriend, and she said yes. After two weeks of sitting together on the bus and sitting next to each other at lunch at school, the relationship was beginning to feel real. The first big date was coming up fast because this weekend was David's fourteenth birthday.

Ally felt excited and went to her friend's house to get ready (fix their hair) before her dad would pick up Ally and her friend and take them to David's house. Their entire friend-group would be there!

When Ally was dropped off, David did a good job of greeting the parents, He introduced himself, said his name clearly, and shook hands firmly and politely with both parents. He spent the whole introductory time standing next to his parents, speaking, and making eye contact with Ally's parents, not moving toward, looking at, or speaking to Ally.

Even when Ally's parents were leaving, it was David's mother who invited the relationally timid and sensitive Ally to join the others downstairs, while David was distracted and responding to one of his other friends.

Two times that evening, Ally felt hurt by David's actions. Once was when a game was played where everyone had to pair up, and he chose to pair up with his long-time friend Mark. The other time was when people were around the firepit at the beach making S'mores. All the other couples were working together making their S'mores and sitting next to one another. David chose to sit across the fire from Ally, and by default she teamed up with her friend, who saw her disappointment and sat next to her.

When Ally's dad showed up to get her, David had left the beach and was playing basketball with his friends, while Ally was still at the fire pit. Rather than go and get Ally, David sent another friend, Tina, to get her. When Ally passed David, she lingered for a moment, but he did not say anything to her, so she walked alone to the car.

When her father got in the car, he asked, "So, how was the party?" He knew all too well that the answer would be a single word: "Fine" (curt and without any tonal inflection).

David gave no Greeting to Ally.
What should he have done or said:

(☐ Relaxed Humor, ☐ Respectful Conviction,
☐ Relational Warmth, ☐ Reasonable Intellect,
☐ Reflective Space, ☐ Responsive Energy)

How many Goal Moments did David miss?
What should he have done?

(☐Closer, ☐Companion, ☐Collaborator, ☐Commander)

David obviously missed the Goodbye.
What should he have said or done?

(☐ Relaxed Humor, ☐ Respectful Conviction,
☐ Relational Warmth, ☐ Reasonable Intellect,
☐ Reflective Space, ☐ Responsive Energy)

Story 3: Deaf and Mute Team-Player

Randy is the Operations Manager for a small non-profit organization that mobilizes the collection of clothing for the poor. Out of a desire to keep overhead to a minimum, the organization uses volunteers to get things done. Stephen is one such volunteer. Stephen came highly recommended for his accounting skills and soon fixed all their cash flow and accounting problems.

Randy, however, is unhappy because Stephen does not ever respond to emails, or texts. Even telephone calls don't get returned. Randy was told up front that Stephen was quiet and didn't respond to pressure, but this lack of response was ridiculous. Randy has always been exceedingly polite and soft spoken, but he does communicate urgency for the things he needs.

Randy has resorted to communicating through Stephen's wife to get information. Which, until recently, was working, but now she has said she is fed up with being the middleman, that Randy's demands are creating too much stress for Stephen. She says that if the two men can't get on the same page, then Stephen should quit!

Getting accounting and status information around financial things has become so difficult that Randy is about to suggest to the President that they release Stephen from his position.

What types of interaction have *not* been happening?

Greeting: (☐ Relaxed Humor, ☐ Respectful Conviction, ☐ Relational Warmth, ☐ Reasonable Intellect, ☐ Reflective Space, ☐ Responsive Energy)

Goal: (☐Closer, ☐Companion, ☐Collaborator, ☐Commander)

Goodbye: (☐ Relaxed Humor, ☐ Respectful Conviction, ☐ Relational Warmth, ☐ Reasonable Intellect, ☐ Reflective Space, ☐ Responsive Energy)

Story 4: Fighting the Right Fight

Dan leads a company of 625 employees, sixty-five in managerial positions with seven direct reports, and half of his problems come from two people.

- Phil verbalizes respect to leadership perspectives, but he does not follow through with the necessary action. Every time there is a lack of follow-through, it comes down to Phil saying that he just didn't see things that way. While Phil is easy to get along with, he is also very logical, analytical, and very talented. Every conversation goes smoothly; even conversations about Phil's lack of performance go smoothly. That is: smoothly for everyone but Tom, who also reports to Dan.
- Tom shows disdain for most leadership perspectives, especially corrective ones about his attitudes, but eventually Tom complies with the necessary action. Every conversation with Tom is difficult with lots of tension and raised voices. even congratulatory conversations (after he obeys) are fraught with tension due to his expression method. Tom is both opinionated and stubborn, but he is also very talented.

If you are Dan how would you coach these two critical employees in their communication?

Coaching for Phil (Who Is Agreeable but Unchangable)

Greeting: (☐ Relaxed Humor, ☐ Respectful Conviction, ☐ Relational Warmth, ☐ Reasonable Intellect, ☐ Reflective Space, ☐ Responsive Energy)

Goal: (☐Closer, ☐Companion, ☐Collaborator, ☐Commander)

Goodbye: (☐ Relaxed Humor, ☐ Respectful Conviction, ☐ Relational Warmth, ☐ Reasonable Intellect, ☐ Reflective Space, ☐ Responsive Energy)

Coaching for Tom (Who Is Contentious but Compliant)

Greeting: (☐ Relaxed Humor, ☐ Respectful Conviction, ☐ Relational Warmth, ☐ Reasonable Intellect, ☐ Reflective Space, ☐ Responsive Energy)

Goal: (☐ Closer, ☐ Companion, ☐ Collaborator, ☐ Commander)

Goodbye: (☐ Relaxed Humor, ☐ Respectful Conviction, ☐ Relational Warmth, ☐ Reasonable Intellect, ☐ Reflective Space, ☐ Responsive Energy)

Chapter FIVE
"Easter Eggs" for Relational Growth, a Baker's Dozen

In computer games there are often hidden nuggets containing information or skills that enable the player to play at a higher level, and these are called Easter Eggs. This chapter contains a baker's dozen of these nuggets of truth learned through thirty-plus years of helping people get along and perform at higher levels.

Figure 21: A Bakers Dozen

Egg #1 STOP (Self-Control)

I was in a team meeting doing a training on management and had a woman say, "I think, to be taken seriously, sometimes you just have to completely lose your sh——."

I couldn't disagree more. I believe there is no quicker way to lose your influence with others than to demonstrate a complete lack of self-control. Anger as a form of influence is completely counterproductive. People with any level of self-respect would not submit to that in their leaders. Such behavior certainly does not generate respect. Instances like that are always used to justify additional wrong actions, and they are never used to justify right actions.

Egg #2 Know Yourself

You see the world through a lens that distorts reality like a fun-house mirror. That lens is your own perceptions and experiences. Without a knowledge of yourself, you will not be likely to spot the distortions that bend your perceptions of reality. Many of the things that make our life seem so hurtful to us are coming from our own mind. With a different set of perceptions, the same circumstances might be interpreted in a vastly less hurtful way, and perhaps not even as a setback but rather as an opportunity.

When you are in a relationship with someone, you do not see them. You perceive them through the lens of yourself (us). Armed with a knowledge of how you see the world (me), you can subtract those viewpoints from your perception of the situation, and then you can see the other person as they truly are (you).

Therefore, the simple equation for understanding another person is: Us – Me = You

You should consider doing this until the other person's actions seem reasonable, because most people have reasons for the things they do.

Egg #3 Be Mindful

You may have heard the word mindfulness thrown around in recent years attached to yoga, meditation, and other eastern religious perspectives. In reality, mindfulness is an old biblical idea with new packaging. The idea is that some part of your conscious mind should be reserved to monitor your well-being and warn you when: you are not being the person you desire to be or living the way you want to live. The psychological version of this concept was packaged by Sigmund Freud as a function of the superego. The Bible called it your conscience.

In any case, this is a part of your mind that stores your highest version of how you should live and logically judges your actions by that code. The mantra to "be mindful" would be equivalent to "live conscientiously" or live with a conscious regard for your best self. It is not unlike Egg #2 (know yourself), but while "know yourself" focuses on your patterns and desires, "be mindful" focuses on *your current emotional state of mind*.

Let's say you believe that the best version of you is one where you are kind. Mindfulness challenges you to be aware of yourself to a point that you immediately feel it when you are drawn away from the kindness you aspire to have in your thoughts and feelings. It would then be up to the strength of your habit concerning Egg #1 (self-control) to stop yourself from progressing into unkindness.

Egg #4 Cut Loose Your Anchors!

The Easter Eggs contain information or skills that help you operate at a higher level. This Egg exemplifies what an Easter Egg does. As mentioned in the Separation Step section of the Emotional House, unresolved emotional pain (an anchor) creates a hardened set of perspectives that damage other relationships, both existing and future. And yet, we often feel less anxiety by creating ways to put up with or shut ourselves away from painful realities than we feel by confronting ourselves with the idea that we have allowed someone to determine our life-satisfaction by their actions.

Egg #4 is an encouragement to act for the benefit of your well-being, your freedom, and your peace. Put your heart in a permanent place of rest concerning your past. Walk up the steps to the freedom of innocence. It's not about having a relationship with the person involved in your painful experience; it's about having the freedom to relate to *anyone* without the shadow of fear and pain from the past looming over you! Life is hard enough looking forward! Looking into your past all the time only increases the likelihood that you will have another painful, emotional accident.

I have met so many unhappy people burdened by pain from their past, and I have often been ruled by the pain of the past myself. As a result, I can testify that no amount of struggle to gain peace is too large of a price to pay. Cut loose your anchors!

Egg #5 Give Grace

The person who trained me to counsel once told me the answer to the question "Why?" is usually very dissatisfactory. I didn't believe her at the time—I was twenty—but by the age of twenty-five I knew beyond a shadow of a doubt that she was right. Thank you, Elisabeth!

Everyone has a "Why" for everything they do, and arguing their "Why" against your "Why" is as fruitless an effort as you will ever attempt. In light of this, if you can live without knowing their "Why"; if you can just assume it is different from yours and be OK with that; if you can set aside the issue of right and wrong and just see people who want to have relationship to you; if you can be good to them because you want to be and not measure it out in proportion to how they have treated you, then *do it*!

Let the struggle for justice go to the God who is the Judge of the living and the dead. Let the struggle for the truth go to the God who is truth. Let go of the struggle for what is loving; leave that to the God who is love. Let go of the struggle for peace; leave that to the God who is the Prince of Peace. Let go of the struggle for joy; leave that to the God of all joy. Let go of the struggle for greatness; leave that to the God of all glory.

When you are struggling to conform others to your perception of these things, you are not letting God be God over both of you! God has the truth of the matter. God knows what is just, and he is not ultimately thwarted in its execution. God has unlimited love for you; you don't need it from someone else. God has peace that surpasses understanding. God has joy unlimited that can be the wellspring of your life. God is the bestower and true defender of all glory, so you don't need to prove anything to anyone but him.

Cease your struggle to bring about these things on a human level by human effort, and abide in the presence of the One who can do all these things. After receiving them in unmeasurable quantity, give them unstintingly. Mercy involves getting something far better than you deserve, and finding grace involves receiving a gift. Giving grace means that you give the good you can, because you can, not because people have earned it or deserve it.

Egg #6 Be "the Good"

When it comes to childrearing there is a big debate about what you should teach your children. Some believe you should teach them realism. Teach them the *current* condition of the world. The world is a tough place (not arguable), so you should be tough on them so they can learn to thrive in that toughness.

Other parents say teach them altruism. Teach them the *future* condition of the world (the world as it could be). The world is becoming a better place (not arguable), so you should be good to them, so they can learn to be the good in the world. Both childrearing viewpoints can be argued as valid, beneficial, and true.

What I have found is that this extends far beyond childrearing into the realm of adult relationships. These viewpoints produce radically different relational impacts. The truth is that most of the time realism means your hope should be tempered with negativity (or skepticism) in order to produce less disappointment when the inevitable failures happen. Whatever you believe about realism as a life perspective, as a relational perspective realism is counterproductive.

Entering a relationship with pessimistic shadows on your outlook—whether from past experiences such as anchors or from realism in your worldview—inhibits you and triggers the guarded response typical for the Judgment Step in your relational House. This makes it easier for you to go *down* the steps than to go *up* the steps with others. It can be so deeply ingrained in you that you do not naturally pursue relationships and call yourself a introvert, a concept never scientifically proven to be a trait even by those who call it such.

Egg #7 Be Curious

Curiosity is not just one of the core stimuli for romance; it is one of the core elements for relational connection of all sorts. Building a healthy curiosity about others drives you to seek their perspectives, to see their reactions, and to desire their participation because it enhances your own. Don't just be curious about the universe around you. Also be curious about the most fascinating part of the universe, the people around you! Humans are herd animals. They are built for communion with each other, and the fullness of living is found in the diversity of the human community.

So, to seek the fullness of living, we must be curious about humanity's thoughts, emotions, reactions, beliefs, aspirations, and reflections. Curiosity is the inspiration to see life from more than one viewpoint. Mark Twain wrote, "To get the full value of a joy you must have someone to divide it with." Without curiosity we fall prey to increasing myopia and self-absorption that inhibit relationships and relational satisfaction.

Egg #8 Think about "The Box"

Some say think outside the box, but this Egg prompts you to recognize that The Box is (relationally speaking) often used as another way of limiting others (or ourselves) to make us feel more comfortable. Recognizing limits is a good thing! People *do not have* unlimited choices; they choose within frameworks. You can't (simply by choosing) do anything or be anything, so it is imperative, if you wish to live purposefully and with awareness of yourself, to know what frameworks you are living within. You also need to know where the limits and weaknesses of those mental, moral, and emotional boundaries are.

In addition, these boundaries that you have are constantly creeping along and being stretched or enforced by experiences. Knowing this about yourself and being aware of these boundaries in others helps you relate with less friction. Or in some cases, you relate only the friction that is necessary for you to maintain the level of perceived autonomy you desire.

While Egg#2 (know yourself) is about knowing who you are (and desire to be), this Egg is about knowing that your self-definition has limits, and those limits are vulnerable. They can be changed by others if you do not maintain boundaries. Moreover, this Egg is about knowing that your actions are probably shaping the experiences and testing the boundaries that belong to other people's self-perceptions. This constant bumping into boundaries produces the give-and-take influence we feel from other people's lives in both healthy and unhealthy ways. Think about your Box; think about the other person's Box; and think about a Box where you can both live in peace.

Egg #9 Remove Yourself

Without developing Egg 8 (an understanding of the limits of self and others), you will not be able to do this one. The ability to remain who you desire to be and to live at peace with others is a complicated virtue. Once attained, it will be recognized by others, and people will ask you to help them get along better with others. Here your ability to define yourself, know your limits, know others, and lose anchors (so you can live at peace with others) will fill you with wisdom.

This Egg tells you that to truly help another person you must remove the desire to make them into you. You are in pursuit of growth and maturity, and you have much to tell and show them. But you will cross a line into unhealthy methods and outcomes if you get too drawn into their world and start telling them what you would do. Instead, challenge them with the principles of growth in self-awareness, self-control, and compassionate choice.

Too much ownership of the outcomes in their lives will lead you to rigid practices that can be copied without personal growth. This is the nature of both the legalism and the institutionalization that are faced by those who lead personal change. I have consulted with change-agents in many fields, and they all face the same issue: if they can't create professional distance, they end up making things worse not better. The strength they desire to build ends up becoming codependent or (worse) a despotic adherence to form without the transformational change that would make those forms beneficial.

Egg #10 Balance Sheet

Good business finances have a balance sheet, an overview of all assets and liabilities. Business leaders make decisions with a view to making that balance sheet stronger. This is not a cash-flow perspective (revenue pending, cash in the bank, current expenses); this is the larger view of overall organizational value. A balance sheet presents the viewpoint that says: if I were to stop this company today and liquidate everything, what would be the financial outcome? Would I have more money or less money than I had when I started this investment?

Life and relationships have this same perspective. The classic Christmas season movie, *It's a Wonderful Life*, is about a person who gets to experience the Balance Sheet perspective on his life (with some divine help). Good businesses use their balance sheet to make business decisions.

Egg #10 encourages you to make relational life choices from a balance-sheet perspective. Is this person going to help me be the person I aspire to be? Will my relational world become stronger because of them? The relational equivalent of the cash flow statement would have you ask if you are benefiting from them, adding benefit to them, and enjoying the process.

But the balance-sheet questions are bigger. Are they helping me grow, helping me become what I desire to be? Stepping back and periodically asking yourself these balance sheet perspective questions will help you decide how to apportion your time and energy to strengthen your life. The balance sheet is brutally realistic. It contains assets *and* liabilities. The liabilities are as necessary to growth as the assets (sometimes more so), but both need to be identified and understood in order to make good future investments in your relationships, life, and well-being.

Egg #11 Definitions Change

As I write this, it is spring and the trees outside my window are budding out new leaves or flowers. During the summer, they are in full leaf; during the fall, brilliant with color; and during the winter, stark with nakedness. It is easy to get caught up in the current changes of the seasons and miss the fact that just a few years ago that thing I call a tree—that shades a small flowerbed now—was just a twig standing three feet tall out of the dirt.

Figure 22: Potential

People are like this tree. The child that is timid and quiet flourishes out into a gregarious college student with friends all over campus. The obstinate, strong-willed child grows into the driven, well-balanced leader of the football team.

Some changes are less desirable. The couple full of affection and closeness grows apart and divorces. The friend you did everything with will now have little to nothing to do with you for reasons that you may not understand. The thing that is sure is that definitions change.

We can get so caught up in the short view of the change of season that we miss the macro-level changes that bind people and multiply growth or separate people and create pain and misery. This Egg helps remind us to be aware of drift in relationships. It asks us to take into consideration the macro-level changes in those around us. This Egg asks us to celebrate who they *are*, *have been*, and *could be*. It asks us to treat others according to their potential and trajectory, not just their current action.

I have a granddaughter (eleven) who talks nonstop, to the point of frustration at times. Should I only see her as this, or should I temper this with the potential of her gregarious nature? Shouldn't any correction of her talkativeness be presented as a caution concerning the presentation of herself, her acceptance by others, and her possible gain or loss of influence?

Should the employee that takes time deliberating decisions only be seen as an obstruction to progress, or should the potential wisdom that comes from deliberation be considered? This Egg would remind us that relationships are always in seed form, but they will not always remain so. Therefore, we should treat people as much according to their *potential* as we do their actions.

Egg #12 Take a Stand

As a trainer in personal and group dynamics, I understand the role played by the anti-leader or the opposition leader who emerges in any group, but this Egg reminds us that to live fully, we must strive to stand *for* something rather than defining ourselves as *against* something. This is also true around relational dynamics.

People can get *very* caught up in standing against things and people, so much so that they fail to live well with anyone. It is a better course of action to take a stand *for* something, and if that brings you up against others who believe differently, then you can create understanding and bridge gaps through conversation rather than drawing battle lines.

It is also a warning to the perpetual fence rider to remind them that peace is reached through choice and negotiation, not ambiguity and pacifying agreement. From a relational viewpoint, many burgeoning friendships have been destroyed because people were unable to take a stand, or they took a stand *against* someone rather than *for* someone. This Egg seeks to remind us that choice is necessary, and the best choices are *for* not *against*. Choose with good counsel, choose with good facts, choose with good intent, but in the end take a stand!

Egg #13 Failure Isn't Fatal, But Time Can Be

I first heard the term Japanese lettuce inspection in the business context. It was in reference to purposeful time delays on the part of a design group that made unworkable a course of action under consideration by the business development group. The term comes from a movie (*Days of Thunder*), and in the movie it goes like this:

> Now y'all heard of a "Japanese Inspection"? Japanese inspection, you see, when the Japs get in a load of lettuce, they're not sure they wanna let in the country, why they'll just let it sit there on the dock 'til they get good and ready to look at. But by then of course, it's all gone rotten. Ain't nothing left to inspect. You see, lettuce is a perishable item.

The idea behind this term whether in the movie (or in business or any part of life) is that choices are perishable, opportunity has a window (of time) in which it can be taken. Delay making the timely choice, and you might be destroying the opportunity altogether. Sometimes, time proves a decision is worth making because the decision endures through time. But, sometimes, time removes opportunity. Time can be fatal. Not choosing *is* a conscious choice, one that delays action. Delay too long, and you may no longer have the same choice or opportunity.

There is often a window of time for things to be done well. A window for reconciliation before resentment hardens, a window for romantically moving beyond friendship to deeper relationship, a window for the correction of an employee before memory fades or excuses are conjured from the ether. A window to end gossip before it destroys lives, a window of time for every choice, for every person, for every season of life, every issue.

You are not going to know the timing for all your choices. But to understand the timing as often as you can is beneficial. Many things are easier to handle when the consequences are small, but some consequences grow with time, and others shrink with time. Knowing how time is working in your relational choices will help you make them well.

Chapter Six
Epilogue: My Journey as a First Responder

If you are the type of person who is naturally attuned to others and by your natural makeup you give the initial instinctive response to others that they are looking for, if you can get along with everyone, and no one dislikes or rejects you, then this book was not written for you. It was written *about* you!

This book was not written by a "people person," and it is not for those who are. Finding a person who is instinctively good at building relationships (by nature and nurture) is like finding a unicorn. I have a few friends like this and have learned a great deal from them. Most of them do what they do so instinctively they can't even explain what they are doing or why they said what they did! Their first response to anyone in any situation soothes the way to building relational connection and they can't even tell the rest of us how to do it!

I have also marveled at the speed and accuracy with which they can calculate and navigate the heuristic inputs confronting them and seamlessly respond with an invitational response that puts people at ease and invites them to more connection. This book tries to slow down, dismantle, and clarify what you do and tell non-relational people how to approximate it, so they can do better.

From infancy, I was trained to fear everything and be a victim to everyone. As an adult I decided to steamroll over everyone or everything in my way. By the time I was twenty, I was the relational equivalent of a train wreck. It is with the deepest thanks to God, teachers, mentors, and friends that I can say, while the last fifteen years have not been free of conflict, I live my life without ongoing burden or pain (from what conflict there was) and in the freedom and joy of the relationships that I choose to live within. If I can improve, anyone can. I have great hope that you can too, and I hope this book helps.

www.ingramcontent.com/pod-product-compliance
Lightning Source LLC
Chambersburg PA
CBHW030158100526
44592CB00009B/341